JOSEP MARIA JUJOL

JOSEP MARIA
JUJOL

José Llinàs · Jordi Sarrà

TASCHEN

HONG KONG KÖLN LONDON LOS ANGELES MADRID PARIS TOKYO

To stay informed about upcoming TASCHEN titles, please request
our magazine at www.taschen.com/magazine or write to TASCHEN,
Hohenzollernring 53, D-50672 Cologne, Germany, contact@taschen.com,
Fax: +49-221-254919. We will be happy to send you a free copy of our
magazine which is filled with information about all of our books.

Original edition © 1992 Benedikt Taschen Verlag GmbH
Text: José Llinàs
Photos: Jordi Sarrà
Production and layout: Gabriele Leuthäuser, Peter Gössel, Nürnberg
Cover design: Sense/Net, Andy Disl & Birgit Reber, Cologne
Production: Ready-Made, Milan
German translation: Willi Zurbrüggen, Heidelberg
English translation: Karen Williams, London
French translation: Marie-Anne Trémeau-Böhm, Cologne

Printed in Germany
ISBN 978–8228–4406–9

INHALT / CONTENTS / SOMMAIRE

EINFÜHRUNG / INTRODUCTION

Skizzenblatt von 1899 / Sketches from 1899 /
Feuille d'esquisses de 1899

Jujol mit Schulkameraden / Jujol with school-
mates / Jujol avec des camarades d'école

Ich sehe ihn vor mir, wie ihn uns die Nonnen aus dem Stiftshaus von Vilanova i la Geltrú beschrieben haben, die in den ersten Bänken ihrer Kapelle saßen und, staunend wie in einem Kino, dem Mann am Hochaltar zuschauten: Josep Maria Jujol, ein alter Mann bereits (1947), mit dem Rücken zum Betrachter, in der linken Hand die Palette und ein gutes Dutzend Pinsel, von denen er mit der rechten einen nach dem anderen herausgreift und ohne zu zögern nacheinander verschiedene Farben auf den behauenen Marmor des Altars aufträgt, bis dieser in leuchtender Frische erstrahlt.

Oder jung und zuversichtlich in Palma de Mallorca (1910) mit Antoni Gaudí bei der Arbeit in der Kathedrale, wie vom Domherrn Emili Sagristà beschrieben: »Einmal konnte ich die beiden Architekten bei der Arbeit beobachten. Jujol arbeitete bei den hinteren drei Bänken rechts vom Altar, und Don Antoni Gaudí stand auf der siebten oder achten Seitenbank. Jujol trug gerade Farbe auf, hatte aber keinen Farbeimer in der Hand, sondern nur einen tropfenden Pinsel, und fragte immer wieder: ›Geht es so, Don Antoni?‹, und Don Antoni sagte dann, aber oft genug auch, ohne daß er gefragt wurde: ›Gut, Jujol! Großartig!‹, und ähnliche Dinge.«

Josep Maria Jujol wurde 1879 in der Stadt Tarragona geboren, seine Eltern stammten aber vom Land. Sein Vater war Schullehrer und zog, als Jujol neun Jahre alt war, aus beruflichen Gründen mit der Familie nach Gràcia, das damals ein Dörfchen und dem ausgreifenden Barcelona noch nicht einverleibt war, und später endgültig in die Innenstadt von Barcelona.

Jujol fühlte sich jedoch zeitlebens der ländlichen Heimat seiner Eltern verbunden, und seine — stark gefühlsmäßige — Beziehung zu diesem Landstrich sollte für die Entwicklung seiner Architektur bestimmend sein.

I see him just as he appeared to the nuns of Vilanova i la Geltrú convent, transfixed in the front pews of their chapel as they glued their eyes, as if to the cinema screen, to the man at the high altar: Josep Maria Jujol, an old man now (1947), stands with his back to the viewer; in his left hand he holds his palette and a good dozen brushes, from which his right hand selects one brush after another to apply an unhesitating succession of different colours to the carved marble of the altar, until it sparkles with radiant freshness.

Or young and confident in Palma de Mallorca (1910), working with Antoni Gaudí inside the cathedral, as described by canon Emili Sagristà: »Once I was able to observe the two architects at work. Jujol was working near the rear three pews (to the right of the altar), and Don Antoni Gaudí was standing on the sixth or seventh side pew. Jujol was in the middle of painting, although he wasn't carrying a paint pot, just a dripping paintbrush, and kept asking: ›Is this all right, Don Antoni?‹. Don Antoni would then say – as indeed he often said even without being asked - ›Good, Jujol! Magnificent!‹ and suchlike things.«

Josep Maria Jujol was born in 1879 in the city of Tarragona, although his parents came from the country. His father was a schoolteacher, who for career reasons moved with the family to Gràcia when Jujol was nine years old. Gràcia was at that time still a village, and not yet incorporated into Greater Barcelona. The family later moved again, permanently, into the centre of Barcelona proper. Jujol nevertheless felt bound all his life to his parents' native countryside, and his – strongly emotional – relationship with their home region was to exert a decisive influence over the development of his architecture.

Je le vois devant moi, tel que l'ont décrit les religieuses du couvent de Vilanova i la Geltrú assises sur les premiers bancs de leur chapelle et regardant avec étonnement, comme au cinéma, l'homme près du maître-autel: Josep Maria Jujol, déjà un vieil homme (1947), tournant le dos au spectateur, dans la main gauche une palette et une bonne douzaine de pinceaux qu'il prend l'un après l'autre avec la main droite, appliquant successivement sans hésiter diverses couleurs sur le marbre taillé de l'autel, jusqu'à ce que celui-ci resplendisse dans sa lumineuse fraîcheur.

Ou bien encore jeune et confiant à Palma de Majorque (1910) avec Antoni Gaudí, travaillant dans la cathédrale, tel que l'a décrit le chanoine Emili Sagristà: »Un jour, j'ai pu observer les deux architectes au travail. Jujol travaillait près des trois bancs du fond (à droite de l'autel), et Don Antoni Gaudí était perché sur le septième ou huitième banc latéral. Jujol était en train d'étaler de la couleur; il n'avait pas de pot de peinture à la main, seulement un pinceau dégouttant, et demandait sans cesse: ›Est-ce que ça va comme ça, Don Antoni?‹ Et Don Antoni disait alors, mais aussi sans qu'on le lui ait demandé, ›Bien, Jujol! Formidable!‹, et d'autres choses de ce genre. «

Josep Maria Jujol est né en 1879 dans la ville de Tarragone, mais ses parents venaient de la campagne. Son père était maître d'école et alla s'installer avec sa famille, alors que Jujol avait neuf ans, à Gràcia, qui était alors un village pas encore rattaché à Barcelone, puis définitivement dans le centre de Barcelone pour des raisons professionnelles.

Toutefois, Jujol se sentit toute sa vie lié à la campagne natale de ses parents, et ses rapports – fortement intuitifs – avec cette région devaient être décisifs pour l'évolution de son architecture.

Schließlich ist es das Hinterland von Tarragona – die Casa Bofarull in Els Pallaresos, die Kirche von Vistabella, das Heiligtum der Heiligen Jungfrau von Montserrat in Montferri – in dem sich uns sein Werk wie eine geöffnete Hand entgegenstreckt, in deren Handfläche wir Steine, landwirtschaftliche Geräte, kleine Tiere und Formen – vielleicht von den Veränderungen dahinziehender Wolken inspiriert – erkennen, die uns das Außergewöhnliche dieser ländlichen Alltagswelt vor Augen führen.

1896 begann Jujol in Barcelona mit dem Architekturstudium, obwohl er sich offenbar seiner Neigung und Eignung nach mehr zu den technischen Fächern hingezogen fühlte und vor der Familie den Wunsch äußerte, die Laufbahn eines Industrieingenieurs einzuschlagen. Auf Anraten seines Vaters, der wirtschaftliche Überlegungen ins Feld führte, studierte er jedoch Architektur. 1906 beendete er das Studium mit herausragenden Leistungen sowohl in den technischen als auch in allen übrigen Fächern.

Wie viele andere Architekten fand Jujol die wesentlichen Impulse seiner beruflichen Bildung wohl weniger an der Hochschule als in den Werkstätten von Antoni Maria Gallissà, in denen er seit 1899 mitarbeitete; 1903 begann seine Zusammenarbeit mit Josep Font i Gumà und ab 1906, nach Abschluß seines Studiums, arbeitete er mit Antoni Gaudí.

Zweifellos lag es an dem Altersunterschied – Gaudí war 27 Jahre älter als Jujol – und an der Erfahrung und dem Ansehen Gaudís, daß diese Zusammenarbeit, die sich mit unterschiedlicher Intensität über Jahre hinzog, für Jujol entschieden mehr bedeutete als für Gaudí. Dennoch ist nicht zu übersehen, wie weit in Gaudís Arbeiten die Handschrift Jujols erkennbar bleibt: Wenn die Hand in Bewegung gerät, wenn der Zufall in die geordneten Geometrien des Meisters einbricht und die Materialien ihr Eigenleben führen, dann war Jujol am Werk.

Indeed, it is in the Tarragona hinterland – in the Casa Bofarull in Els Pallaresos, the church in Vistabella, the shrine to the Blessed Virgin of Montserrat in Montferri – that his work beckons to us most clearly, like an outstretched hand in whose palm we recognize stones, agricultural implements, animals and forms, perhaps inspired by the changing shapes of passing clouds, which together reveal the miraculous dimension of everyday rural life.

In 1896 Jujol began studying architecture in Barcelona, although he apparently felt more strongly drawn by aptitude and personal preference to the technological field, and told his family that he wished to pursue a career as an industrial engineer. Upon the advice of his father, however, who argued the financial advantages, he settled for architecture. He completed his studies in 1906, having achieved outstanding grades in every subject.

Jujol, like so many other architects, found his most profound inspiration less in his academic environment than in the practical experience which he gained under such masters as Antoni Maria Gallissà, in whose studio he was employed as from 1899, Josep Font i Gumà, with whom he worked as from 1903, and Antoni Gaudí, with whom he collaborated after completing his studies in 1906. The large age gap – Gaudí was 27 years older than Jujol –, coupled with Gaudí's experience and reputation, no doubt explains why this last collaboration – which continued with varying degrees of intensity over many years – was considerably more significant for Jujol than for Gaudí. The extent to which Jujol's signature is recognizable in Gaudí's work cannot be overlooked, however; wherever the hand is set in motion, wherever chance invades the ordered geometries of the master and materials disperse – there Jujol is at work.

C'est finalement dans l'arrière-pays de Tarragone – la Casa Bofarull à Els Pallaresos, l'église de Vistabella, le sanctuaire de la sainte Vierge de Montserrat à Montferri –, que son œuvre se tend vers nous comme une main ouverte dans laquelle nous reconnaissons des pierres, des outils agricoles, des petits animaux et des petites formes, peut-être inspirées par les transformations des nuages qui passent, qui nous montrent le caractère extraordinaire de ce monde agreste de tous les jours.

En 1896, Jujol commence à étudier l'architecture à Barcelone, bien qu'il se sente apparemment plus attiré, de par ses goûts et ses capacités, par les matières techniques et exprime devant sa famille le désir de devenir ingénieur industriel. Sur le conseil de son père, qui avance des réflexions économiques, Jujol étudie toutefois l'architecture. En 1906, il termine ses études avec d'excellents résultats aussi bien dans les matières techniques que dans toutes les autres.

De même que beaucoup d'autres architectes, Jujol trouve les impulsions essentielles de sa formation professionnelle moins à l'université que dans les ateliers d'Antoni Maria Gallissà, où il travaille depuis 1899, de Josep Font i Gumà, à partir de 1903, de même que dans la collaboration avec Antoni Gaudí, à partir de 1906, après avoir terminé ses études. Sans aucun doute, la différence d'âge – Gaudí avait 27 ans de plus que Jujol –, l'expérience et la célébrité de Gaudí sont cause que cette collaboration, qui s'étend sur plusieurs années avec une intensité variable, signifie beaucoup plus pour Jujol que pour Gaudí. Il ne faut cependant pas oublier dans quelle mesure la signature de Jujol est reconnaissable dans les œuvres de Gaudí: quand la main se met en mouvement, quand le hasard fait irruption dans les géométries ordonnées du maître et quand les matériaux contrastent, c'est que Jujol était à l'œuvre.

Bebauungsentwurf für Les Corts, 1913 / Development plan for Les Corts, 1913 / Plan d'aménagement pour Les Corts, 1913

Mosaikentwurf für die Casa Escofet, 1910 / Design for a mosaic in the Casa Escofet, 1910 / Projet de mosaïque pour la Casa Escofet, 1910

So war Jujol für die Keramikauflage der langen geschwungenen Bänke und die Ausarbeitung der Decke der Säulenhalle des Park Güell verantwortlich. Das Material, das er dort verwendete – in Stücke gebrochene Fliesen, Teller, Tassen, Flaschen, Gläser, Krüge und ähnliches –, war zum großen Teil Ausschuß und Abfallmaterial, Auswahl und Zusammenstellung also abhängig von der Zufälligkeit des Vorgefundenen. Aus Scherben ein Mosaik zu gestalten oder, allgemein ausgedrückt, unbrauchbar Gewordenes, Weggeworfenes wiederzuverwerten ist eine Konstante in Jujols Arbeitsweise, die Kartons zu Konsolen werden läßt, landwirtschaftliches Gerät zu Gitterwerk verarbeitet, Feldsteine für Friese und Gesimse einsetzt und aus Konservendosen Lampenrosetten formt.

Die Keramikarbeiten an der Fassade der Casa Batlló scheint Jujol nach Ideen Gaudís realisiert zu haben. Im ersten Stock ist sein Einfluß außerdem deutlich an der Ausführung der Türen erkennbar. Auch die Zimmerdecken und die Säulen im ersten Stock der Casa Milà stammen von Jujol; und obwohl es nicht hinlänglich bewiesen ist und es wohl auch widersprüchliche Aussagen darüber gibt, gilt das für mich genauso für die schmiedeeisernen Geländer, die in jedem Fall ein Gaudí/Jujol zuzuschreibendes Wunderwerk sind.

Der Architekt und Historiker Carlos Flores war einer der ersten, die Jujol Anerkennung zuteil werden ließen, und gilt als der beste Interpret seines Werkes. Er hat eine großartige Beschreibung der Persönlichkeit und Arbeit beider Architekten verfaßt, aus der ich einige Passagen zitieren möchte:

»Seit Jujol in Gaudís Werken vertreten ist, wird in ihnen eine Veränderung spürbar, die über jene konkreten Bereiche, die Jujol innerhalb dieses Werkes persönlich ausführt, hinausgeht.«

Thus Jujol was responsible for the decorative ceramics revetting the serpentine park seating and the ceiling of the columned hall in Park Güell. The materials which he employed – broken tiles, plates, cups, bottles, glasses, jugs, etc. – were largely rejects and waste materials. Selection and combination were thus dictated by their random nature. Creating a mosaic out of waste ceramics and indeed waste recycling in general, is a constant of the Jujol work ethic, which builds consoles out of cardboard boxes, reworks farmyard equipment into a grille, employs fieldstones as mouldings and turns tin cans into lamp rosettes.

Jujol appears to have executed the ceramics on the façade of the Casa Batlló after ideas by Gaudí. His influence is also clearly visible in the execution of the doors on the first floor. The ceilings and columns on the first floor of the Casa Milà also stemmed from Jujol. And while it may still remain inadequately proven and the subject of conflicting claims, the same is true – in my view, certainly – of the wrought-iron banisters, a miracle attributable at all events to the Gaudí/Jujol partnership.

The architect and historian Carlos Flores was one of the first to acknowledge the significance of Jujol's architectural contribution, and ranks as the finest interpreter of his œuvre. He has authored an excellent description of the personalities and works of both architects, from which I would like to cite a few passages below:

»Since Jujol has featured in Gaudí's works, a change has become perceptible in them which goes beyond those specific areas which Jujol personally executes.«

Jujol était responsable de la couche de céramique des longs bancs incurvés et de l'élaboration du plafond du portique du Parc Güell. Les matériaux qu'il employa à cet effet – assiettes, tasses, bouteilles, verres, cruches et choses semblables – étaient en grande partie rebut et déchets, si bien que son travail consistait à choisir et à combiner et dépendait donc du hasard des matériaux trouvés. Créer une mosaïque avec des tessons ou, pour généraliser, réutiliser des pièces devenues inutiles et mises au rebut est une constante dans la méthode de travail de Jujol, qui transforme des cartons en corbeaux, utilise des outils agricoles pour faire une grille, emploie des pierres de taille pour des frises et des corniches, et forme des rosettes de lampe avec des boîtes de conserve.

Jujol semble avoir réalisé les céramiques de la façade de la Casa Battlò d'après des idées de Gaudí. Au premier étage, on reconnaît en outre clairement son influence à l'exécution des portes. Les plafonds et la réalisation des colonnes du premier étage de la Casa Milà ont été également exécutés par Jujol; et bien que cela ne soit pas suffisamment prouvé et qu'il y ait également des déclarations contradictoires à ce sujet, cela est aussi valable à mon avis pour les balustrades en fer forgé qui sont en tout cas une merveille attribuable à Gaudí et à Jujol. L'architecte et historien Carlos Flores a été l'un des premiers à reconnaître le mérite de Jujol et est considéré comme le meilleur interprète de son œuvre. Il a magnifiquement décrit la personnalité et le travail des deux architectes, et je voudrais citer quelques passages de son essai:

»Depuis que Jujol est représenté dans les œuvres de Gaudí, on y remarque un changement allant au-delà des domaines concrets que Jujol réalise personnellement à l'intérieur de cette œuvre. «

Lüster aus der Kirche von Vistabella / Lustre from the Church of Vistabella / Lustre de l'église de Vistabella

Möbelskizzen / Furniture sketches / Esquisses
de meubles

»Jujol is unanimously described as a thoroughly modest man, one who left barely a trace as he passed through life, but whose creative expression possessed an explosive power. His commissions came not, as in the case of Gaudí, from bishops and distinguished society, but from village priests and minor industrialists.«

»Attention has previously been drawn only to the admiration and indeed enthusiasm which Gaudí felt for Jujol's work. The fact has been ignored, in my view unjustifiably, that Jujol at times approached the work passed on to him by Gaudí with such determination, unceremoniousness and unwillingness to compromise that it astonished and at times infuriated even the master himself.«

By way of conclusion to these observations on the Gaudí-Jujol relationship, a few words by Gaudí himself, prompted by a request from the church governing body in Palma to account for Jujol's behaviour during work on the cathedral: »I have two cats in the house: one, Sugranyes, does his work where he's supposed to do it; the other, Jujol, does it precisely where he shouldn't. You are completely right, but what can I do?«

In 1927, after an engagement lasting several years, Jujol – now 48 years old – married his much younger cousin Teresa Gibert. In January 1928 the couple set off on a three-week holiday to Rome. So enthralled were they by the Eternal City, however, that their three weeks became two months. It was the only trip that Jujol was ever to make beyond the borders of Catalonia.

For Jujol, »to whom work by the hour and wages by the hour were previously unknown«, there now began a period in which family duties went hand in hand with a noticeable increase in professional activity.

»Conformément à des déclarations concordantes, Jujol était quelqu'un de tout à fait modeste, quelqu'un qui n'a guère laissé de traces derrière lui dans la vie, bien que son expression créatrice ait eu une force explosive. Ses commanditaires n'étaient pas, comme ceux de Gaudí, des évêques et des messieurs distingués, mais des curés de campagne et des petits fabricants.«

»Jusqu'ici, on a uniquement souligné l'admiration et l'estime que Gaudí vouait à l'œuvre de Jujol. D'une façon qui me semble injustifiée, on a cependant passé sous silence jusqu'ici que, dans les travaux qui lui étaient confiés par Gaudí, Jujol procédait à l'occasion avec une telle détermination, un tel sans-gêne et une telle inflexibilité, que le maître en était étonné et parfois même outré.«

Pour terminer ces notes relatives aux rapports Gaudí-Jujol, citons encore quelques mots prononcés par Gaudí en personne, quand la direction de l'église de Palma lui demanda de rendre compte de l'attitude de Jujol pendant les travaux de la cathédrale: »J'ai deux chats à la maison: l'un, Sugranyes, fait son travail là où il doit le faire; l'autre, Jujol, le fait là où il n'a nullement le droit de le faire. Vous avez parfaitement raison, mais que voulez-vous que je fasse?«

Après de longues fiançailles, Jujol – âgé maintenant de 48 ans – épouse en 1927 sa cousine Teresa Gibert qui est beaucoup plus jeune que lui. En janvier 1928, tous deux entreprennent un voyage de trois semaines en direction de Rome. Ils sont tellement enthousiasmés par la ville éternelle qu'ils y restent deux mois au lieu des trois semaines prévues. Cela devait être l'unique voyage entrepris par Jujol au-delà des frontières de la Catalogne.

Pour Jujol »pour qui le travail à l'heure et les honoraires étaient jusque-là inconnus«, commence alors une époque pendant laquelle ses devoirs familiaux naturels s'accompagnent d'un remarquable accroissement de son activité professionnelle.

»Übereinstimmenden Aussagen zufolge war Jujol ein ganz und gar bescheidener Mensch, einer, der kaum eine Spur im Leben hinterließ, obwohl sein gestalterischer Ausdruck von explosiver Kraft war. Seine Auftraggeber waren nicht, wie bei Antoni Gaudí, Bischöfe und vornehme Herren, sondern Dorfpfarrer und Kleinfabrikanten.«

»Bisher wurde immer nur hervorgehoben, welche Bewunderung oder gar Begeisterung Gaudí für Jujols Arbeit empfand. Auf eine uns ungerechtfertigt erscheinende Weise ist jedoch bisher verschwiegen worden, daß Jujol bei den ihm von Gaudí übertragenen Arbeiten gelegentlich mit einer solchen Entschlossenheit, Ungeniertheit und Kompromißlosigkeit zu Werke ging, daß es selbst den Meister erstaunt und ab und zu wohl empört hat.«

Zum Abschluß dieser Notizen über das Verhältnis Gaudí/Jujol noch ein paar Worte von Gaudí selbst, als er von der Kirchenleitung in Palma aufgefordert wurde, Rechenschaft über Jujols Verhalten bei den Arbeiten an der Kathedrale abzulegen: »Ich habe zwei Kater im Haus: Einer, Sugranyes, macht seine Arbeit dort, wo er sie machen soll; der andere, Jujol, macht sie da, wo er sie gar nicht machen darf. Sie haben vollkommen recht, aber was soll ich tun?«

1927 heiratete Jujol – inzwischen 48 Jahre alt – nach mehrjähriger Verlobungszeit seine sehr viel jüngere Cousine Teresa Gibert. Im Januar 1928 brachen die beiden zu einer dreiwöchigen Reise nach Rom auf. Sie waren von der Ewigen Stadt jedoch so begeistert, daß aus den geplanten drei Wochen zwei Monate wurden. Es sollte die einzige Reise bleiben, die Jujol Zeit seines Lebens über die Grenzen Kataloniens hinaus unternahm. Für Jujol, »dem bis dahin Arbeit nach Stunden und Honorare pro Stunde unbekannt waren«, begann nun eine Zeit, in der für ihn selbstverständliche familiäre Aufgaben mit einer bemerkenswerten Zunahme seiner beruflichen Aktivität einhergingen.

Das Ehepaar Jujol / Jujol and his wife / Le couple
Jujol

Brunnen auf der Plaça d'Espanya / Fountain on
the Plaça d'Espanya / Fontaine de la Plaça
d'Espanya

Das nach der Hochzeitsreise vielleicht als Antwort auf seinen neuen Stand und den daraus folgenden finanziellen Erfordernissen begonnene Brunnenprojekt auf der Plaça d'Espanya in Barcelona ist innerhalb des Jujolschen Gesamtwerks als der Versuch zu werten, sich in die institutionelle Architektur einzuführen, und steht im Gegensatz zu den bisherigen recht unspektakulären, bescheidenen und schlecht bezahlten Privataufträgen, die er allerdings ohne jede Zeitbegrenzung, nur nach Lust und Inspiration hatte ausführen können. Der Versuch, eine solche Arbeitsweise bei einem städtischen Auftrag beizubehalten, führte zu allerlei Reibungen und Mißstimmungen: Am 19. Mai 1929, dem Tag der Eröffnung der Weltausstellung, war der Brunnen noch nicht ganz fertig, und bis er als solcher in Betrieb genommen werden konnte, verging weitere Zeit; Jahre später verschwanden Metallteile des Brunnens, und die Stadt trug das Ihre zu seiner Verstümmelung bei, indem sie die Leuchten und andere Teile abmontieren und das Werk so definitiv unvollendet stehen ließ. Die Nachlässigkeit der Stadt zeigte sich auch in der Bezahlung des Honorars, das erst im Jahr 1943 ganz beglichen wurde.

Jujols Werk, das so wenig von kollektiven Strömungen abhängig ist und so sehr von persönlichen Überzeugungen, so wenig von der Architektur als geordneter, akademischer Tätigkeit und so sehr von seiner sensiblen Wahrnehmung der Natur oder der Tradition, so wenig von Konstruktionsverfahren und so sehr von dem, was sich beim Akt des Bauens als Material anbietet – ein solches Werk ist nur schwer mit Bürokratie und Vorschriften in Einklang zu bringen. Gerade das Fehlen von Geld ist der Nährboden, auf dem sein Werk gedeiht, das nicht den geringsten Ehrgeiz hat, Macht zu repräsentieren, das aber bei jeder nur denkbaren Gelegenheit die tiefe Frömmigkeit des Meisters sichtbar werden läßt.

The fountain project in the Plaça d'Espanya in Barcelona begun after his honeymoon, and perhaps prompted by his new status and the financial responsibilities it entailed, may be seen within the overall context of Jujol's œuvre as an attempt to establish himself within the field of institutional architecture. It stands in contrast to his previous private commissions which, although they had been rather modest, unspectacular and badly-paid, had nevertheless allowed him to work at his own speed and according to his own inclination and inspiration. Jujol's adoption of a similar approach towards the execution of a municipal commission led, however, to all sorts of friction and ill feeling. On 19 May 1929, the day of the opening of the International Exhibition, the fountain was still unfinished, and it was some time before it finally went into practical operation. A number of its metal components subsequently went missing some years later, and the fountain's disfigurement was further compounded by the municipal authorities, who removed the lights and other features and thus left the work to stand permanently incomplete. This laxity on the part of the city even extended to the payment of Jujol's fee, which was only finally settled in 1943.

Jujol's work, which depends so little on collective trends and so much on personal convictions, so little on architecture as an ordered, academic activity and so much on a sensitive understanding of nature and tradition, so little on the construction process and so much on what offers itself as material during the act of building, which depends so little on money – and indeed thrives best where money is lacking – and which nurtures not the slightest ambition to reflect worldly power, but which reveals the deep devoutness of the architect at every conceivable opportunity – such work is naturally difficult to reconcile with bureaucracy and regulations.

Le projet de fontaine pour la Plaça d'Espanya à Barcelone, qui fut commencé après le voyage de noces peut-être en réponse à sa nouvelle situation et aux besoins financiers en découlant, doit être considéré dans l'ensemble de l'œuvre de Jujol comme une tentative pour s'initier à l'architecture institutionnelle et contraste avec les commandes privées jusque-là peu spectaculaires, modestes et mal rémunérées qu'il avait à vrai dire pu exécuter sans limite de temps, seulement au gré de sa fantaisie. Sa tentative pour conserver une telle méthode de travail lors d'une commande municipale aboutit à toutes sortes de frictions et de querelles: le 19 mai 1929, jour de l'inauguration de l'exposition universelle, la fontaine n'était pas encore tout à fait terminée, et il se passa encore un certain temps avant qu'elle puisse être mise en service en tant que telle. Quelques années plus tard, des pièces métalliques de la fontaine disparurent, et la ville contribua à sa mutilation en faisant démonter les lampes et d'autres pièces, laissant ainsi l'œuvre définitivement inachevée. La négligence de la ville se manifesta également dans le paiement des honoraires qui furent seulement réglés dans leur intégralité en 1943.

L'œuvre de Jujol, qui dépend si peu des courants collectifs et tant des convictions personnelles, si peu de l'architecture en tant qu'activité réglée, académique, et tant de sa perception sensible de la nature ou de la tradition, qui dépend si peu des méthodes de construction et tant des matériaux qui se présentent au cours de l'acte d'édification, qui dépend si peu de l'argent – c'est justement le manque d'argent qui est le terrain favorable sur lequel pousse son œuvre –, qui n'a pas la moindre prétention de représenter le pouvoir, mais laisse apparaître la profonde piété du maître en toute occasion, est bien entendu difficilement conciliable avec la bureaucratie et les règlements.

Wandleuchte aus der Fabrik Mañach / Wall lamp from the Mañach factory / Applique provenant de la fabrique Mañach

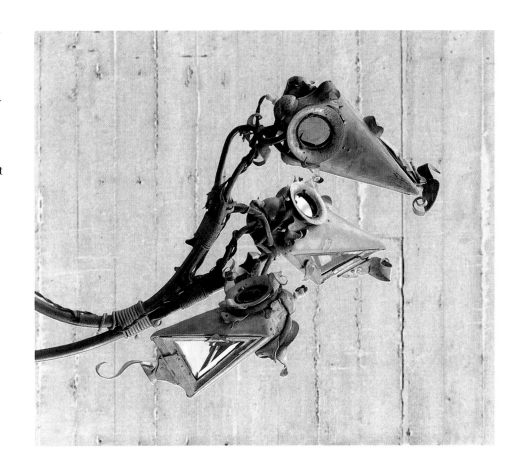

Skizze zum Marienheiligtum in Montferri / Sketch
for the Shrine of the Blessed Virgin in Montferri /
Esquisse pour le sanctuaire marial de Montferri

Das ist wohl die Erkenntnis aus dem, was
als Jujols Versuch gelten kann, einver-
nehmlich mit Behörden zu arbeiten, und
was meiner Meinung nach nur die Au-
ßergewöhnlichkeit und Heterodoxie seines Werkes bestätigt, das absolut unge-
eignet war, dem Staat als Repräsenta-
tionsinstrument zu dienen. Der Brunnen
auf der Plaça d'Espanya markiert vielleicht den Beginn einer zunehmenden
Isolierung und Marginalisierung Jujols in
seinem Verhältnis zu den neu entstande-
nen gesellschaftlichen Kräften Kataloniens; eine Isolation, die bis zu seinem
Tod im Jahre 1949 nicht mehr durchbro-
chen wurde.

In diesem Zusammenhang soll auch darauf hingewiesen werden, daß es nach
dem Ableben Gaudís im Jahre 1926 eigentlich an Jujol gewesen wäre, aufgrund
seiner Nähe zum »Maestro« und der
Dauer und Intensität seiner Zusammenarbeit mit ihm, die Arbeiten an der Sagrada Familia in Barcelona fortzusetzen.
Statt dessen benannten die Stadtväter einen Gehilfen und legten mit dieser Ent-
scheidung den Grundstein dafür, daß die
Arbeit an der Kirche immer weniger ar-
chitektonischen Gesichtspunkten folgte
und sich statt dessen dem Tourismus und
der Politik verschrieb. Sich vorzustellen,
was aus der Sagrada Familia hätte werden können, wenn Jujol mit der Weiter-
führung betraut worden wäre, ist von einer so durchschlagenden Wirkung, daß
dafür ein eigener Lehrstuhl an der Uni-
versität seine Berechtigung hätte.

Tatsächlich arbeitet Jujol nach 1930 nur
noch an kleineren Aufträgen. Der eine
oder andere größere – beispielsweise die
Umbauarbeiten an der Kirche von Roda
de Barà – wird wegen der politischen Er-
eignisse im Land, die ihren Höhepunkt
im Ausbruch des Bürgerkriegs finden,
nicht vollendet oder geht ihm verloren.
Josep Maria Jujol war ein frommer Mann,
der seine Frömmigkeit in solche Extreme
trieb, daß ihm deswegen nach und nach
seine Ämter als Dozent an der Hochschule für Architektur und der Gewerbeschule entzogen wurden und er, wie sein
Sohn in dem Buch »Jujol, un artista completo« schreibt, bei verschiedenen Gele-
genheiten sogar von der Polizei oder
Landgendarmerie abgeholt wurde.

This is surely the conclusion that emerges from what may be seen as Jujol's attempt to work for authority, and what in my opinion simply confirms the extraordinary and heterodox nature of his work, which is totally unsuited to serve as the vehicle of state pomp. The fountain on the Plaça d'Espanya perhaps marks the beginning of the isolation and marginalization which increasingly characterized Jujol's position with relation to Catalonia's newly-emerging social forces – an isolation which was to last until his death in 1949.

In this context it should also be noted that, following Gaudí's death in 1926, the task of continuing work on the church of the Sagrada Familia in Barcelona should rightly have fallen to Jujol, on account of his closeness to the »Maestro« and the length and intensity of their collaboration. But the city fathers appointed a clerk instead, a decision which ultimately resulted in work on the church being governed ever less by architectural considerations and ever more by the dictates of tourism and politics. To imagine what might have become of the Sagrada Familia, had Jujol been entrusted with its completion, is an exercise with such sensational implications as to justify a university chair in its own right.

In reality, however, from 1930 onwards Jujol worked only on smaller projects. Due to the country's political upheavals, which culminated in the outbreak of the Civil War, even the occasional larger commission – such as renovations to the church of Roda de Barà – either remained unfinished or escaped him. Josep Maria Jujol was a pious man, but one who took his piety to such extremes that he gradually lost his posts as lecturer at the College of Architecture and the Technical College. He was even, as his son writes in his book »Jujol, un artista completo«, picked up by the police and rural constabulary a number of times.

C'est peut-être là la découverte de ce qui peut être considéré comme l'essai entrepris par Jujol pour travailler en bonne intelligence avec les autorités et qui, à mon avis, confirme seulement le caractère exceptionnel et l'hétérodoxie de son œuvre, œuvre qui était absolument impropre à servir l'Etat en tant qu'instrument de représentation. La fontaine de la Plaça d'Espanya marque peut-être le début de la marginalisation et de l'isolement croissants de Jujol dans ses rapports avec les forces sociales en voie de formation en Catalogne; un isolement qui ne fut plus rompu jusqu'à sa mort en 1949.

Rappelons à ce propos qu'après le décès de Gaudí en 1926, c'est au fond Jujol qui, parce qu'il était proche du »Maestro« et avait longtemps et intensément collaboré avec ce dernier, aurait dû poursuivre les travaux de la Sagrada Familia à Barcelone. Au lieu de cela, les édiles nommèrent un assistant, justifiant ainsi le fait que les travaux dans l'église suivirent de moins en moins des points de vue architectoniques et se vouèrent à la place au tourisme et à la politique. Imaginer ce qu'il aurait pu advenir de la Sagrada Familia si Jujol avait été chargé de poursuivre les travaux a tant de poids que cela justifierait une chaire personnelle à l'université.

En fait, Jujol ne travaille plus qu'à de petites commandes après 1930. L'une ou l'autre grande commande – par exemple les travaux de transformation de l'église de Roda de Barà – n'est pas achevée ou est abandonnée à cause des évènements politiques qui trouvent leur point culminant lorsqu'éclate la guerre civile. Jujol était un homme pieux qui poussait la piété à de tels extrêmes qu'il fut relevé de ses fonctions de chargé de cours de l'École supérieure d'architecture et de l'École technique pour cette raison et que la police ou la gendarmerie vint même le chercher à plusieurs reprises, comme l'écrit son fils dans le livre »Jujol, un artista completo«.

Man versteht daher, daß Jujol, als der Bürgerkrieg endet, nicht der Verliererseite zugerechnet werden kann; ebensowenig kann man ihn aber zu den Gewinnern zählen, denn in der faschistischen Front hätte er sich gar nicht zurechtgefunden. Sein Mangel an Opportunismus und Lenkbarkeit war dann wohl auch der Grund dafür, daß ihm Aufträge, die seinem Ruf und seiner Erfahrung entsprochen hätten, vorenthalten blieben. Jujol, der seit dem Krieg eine angegriffene Gesundheit hatte und unter enormen finanziellen Schwierigkeiten litt, arbeitete von da an fast nur noch an kleinen Aufträgen religiöser Art, wie Kirchenumbauten und Restaurierungen von Altären und Kapellen, und das bis zu seinem Lebensende. Darin zeigt sich auch die zunehmende Zurückgezogenheit des Architekten und eine abgrundtiefe, unwiderrufliche Abkehr von der geschichtlichen Gegenwart. Trotzdem leuchtet in diesen bescheidenen und oft nicht zu Ende geführten Arbeiten immer wieder ein genialer, heterodoxer Funke auf, der — wie in der Taufkapelle von Bonastre — die Professionalität und Reife eines großen Architekten widerspiegelt.

Jujol unterwegs / Jujol on the road / Jujol en chemin

And while Jujol clearly cannot be included in the losing side at the end of the Civil War, no more can he be numbered amongst the winners, for he would have felt no happier in the Fascist front. His lack of opportunism and manœuvrability was probably also the reason why commissions appropriate to his reputation and experience were withheld from him. Jujol, dogged by poor health and enormous financial worries from the war onwards, worked from now until his death almost exclusively on small commissions of a religious nature, such as church alterations, the restoration of altars and chapels, etc. The architect thereby underlined his increasing seclusion and his unfathomable, irrevocable withdrawal from the historical present. These modest, often unfinished commissions nevertheless continue to reveal regular flashes of heterodox genius, reflecting — as in the baptistry at Bonastre — the professionalism and maturity of a great architect.

On comprend donc que, quand la guerre civile prend fin, Jujol ne peut pas être compté parmi les perdants; on ne peut toutefois pas non plus le compter parmi les gagnants, car il n'aurait pas su comment faire sur le front fasciste. Son manque d'opportunisme et de souplesse est certainement la raison pour laquelle il a été privé de commandes qui auraient correspondu à sa réputation et à son expérience.

Jujol, qui a une santé chancelante et d'énormes difficultés financières depuis la guerre, travaille dès lors presque exclusivement à de petites commandes d'ordre religieux telles que des transformations d'églises et des restaurations d'autels et de chapelles, et ce, jusqu'à sa mort. On voit là aussi la solitude croissante de l'architecte et une aversion profonde et irrévocable pour le présent historique. Une étincelle géniale et hétérodoxe jaillit malgré tout à plusieurs reprises dans ces travaux modestes et souvent inachevés, étincelle qui — comme dans les fonts baptismaux de Bonastre — reflète le professionnalisme et la maturité d'un grand architecte.

AUSGEWÄHLTE WERKE /

SELECTED WORKS / ŒUVRES SELECTIONEES

CASA BATLLO

Passeig de Gràcia 43, Barcelona, 1905–1907
Jujol war Mitarbeiter von Antoni Gaudí bei diesem Projekt / Jujol assisted Antoni Gaudí
on this project / Pour ce projet Jujol travailla avec Antoni Gaudí

CASA MILA

Passeig de Gràcia 92, Barcelona, 1905–1910
Jujol war Mitarbeiter von Antoni Gaudí bei diesem Projekt / Jujol assisted Antoni Gaudí
on this project / Pour ce projet Jujol travailla avec Antoni Gaudí

CATEDRAL DE PALMA

Plaça de la Catedral, Palma de Mallorca, 1903–1914
Jujol war Mitarbeiter von Antoni Gaudí bei diesem Projekt / Jujol assisted Antoni Gaudí
on this project / Pour ce projet Jujol travailla avec Antoni Gaudí

Übermalte Wandvertäfelungen / Painted-over
wall panelling / Lambris peints

PARC GÜELL

Carrer d'Olot, Barcelona, 1900–1914
Jujol war Mitarbeiter von Antoni Gaudí bei diesem Projekt / Jujol assisted Antoni Gaudí
on this project / Pour ce projet Jujol travailla avec Antoni Gaudí

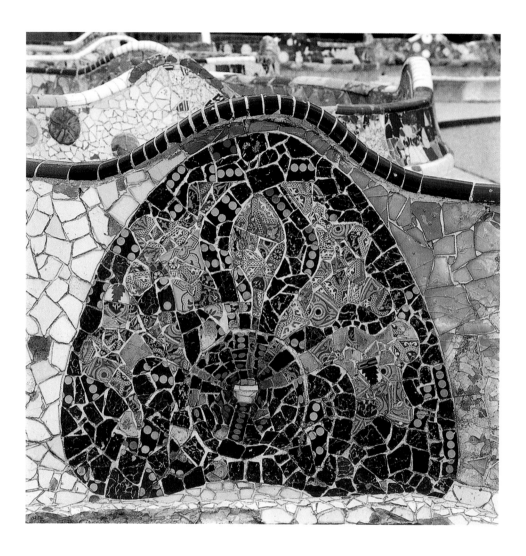

Details der langen geschwungenen Bänke im Park
Güell / Details of the long, undulating benches in
Güell Park / Détails des longs bancs ondulés du
Parque Güell

TEATRE AL PATRONAT OBRER

Theater des Arbeiterpatronats / Theatre of the Workers' Patronage /
Théâtre du patronat ouvrier
Rambla de Sant Joan 46, Tarragona, 1908

Dieses Theater ist eine der ersten Arbeiten Jujols als Architekt und wurde von der katholischen Sozietät »Arbeiterpatronat« in Auftrag gegeben. Allerdings kam es während des Baus zu Meinungsverschiedenheiten mit Mitgliedern der Sozietät, die so weit gingen, daß Jujol die Ausführung nicht mehr beenden konnte. Betroffen waren davon vor allem die Ausmalung, ein paar abschließende Arbeiten und Dekorationen. Noch zu Jujols Lebzeiten fand das Theater als Kino Verwendung, und grundlegende Elemente seiner Arbeit wurden entfernt oder verändert. Später setzte sich dieser Prozeß fort, und das Gebäude wurde immer mehr vernachlässigt.

In dem Buch »Jujol, un artista completo« sagt sein Sohn, daß der Innenraum als Darstellung einer religiösen Allegorie gedacht war: ein Schiff (das Kirchenschiff), in dem die Zuschauer gegen die widrigen Wellen des Lebens kämpfen. Tatsächlich finden sich in dem Theater viele Bezüge zum Meer, denen meiner Meinung nach die Idee zugrunde liegt, den ersten Rang, das heißt, die Etage des Eingangs von der Rambla aus, als die Wasserfläche des Meeres zu sehen. Das Deckengewölbe des Parketts wäre nach dieser These die Wasseroberfläche, von unter Wasser aus betrachtet.

Wenn das Wasser sich an den Felsen bricht, bäumt es sich auf und schäumt empor; genau das scheint das Geländer des ersten Ranges auszudrücken.

This theatre was one of Jujol's commissions as a qualified architect and was executed on behalf of the catholic »Workers' Patronage« society. However, differences of opinion arose with members of the society even while work was in progress, which ultimately resulted in Jujol being unable to complete his work. This particularly affected the painting, a few borders and decorations. The theatre was converted into a cinema during Jujol's own lifetime, and fundamental elements of his work were removed or altered. This process was later continued and the building suffered increasing neglect.

In his book »Jujol, un artista completo« Jujol's son states that the theatre interior was conceived as the religious allegory of a ship (the Church), in which the audience battles against the adverse waves of life. The theatre indeed contains many references to the sea, to our mind centred on the idea that the Dress Circle – the level at which the theatre is entered from the Rambla – should be seen as the surface of the sea. The ceiling of the Stalls would thereby correspond to the surface of the sea as seen from under water.

Water, when it breaks over rocks, surges and froths – precisely what the railings of the Dress Circle seem to express.

Ce théâtre est l'une des premières œuvres réalisées par Jujol en tant qu'architecte et lui fut commandé par la société catholique »Patronat ouvrier«. Pendant la construction, il eut toutefois des différends avec des membres de la société, et cela alla si loin que Jujol ne put achever les travaux. Ceci toucha avant tout la peinture, quelques finitions et décorations. Du vivant de Jujol, le théâtre fut utilisé comme cinéma, et des éléments fondamentaux de son travail furent supprimés ou modifiés. Par la suite, ce processus se poursuivit, et le bâtiment fut de plus en plus négligé.

Dans le livre »Jujol, un artista completo«, le fils de Jujol dit que l'intérieur était conçu comme représentation d'une allégorie religieuse: un bateau (la nef de l'église) dans lequel les spectateurs luttent contre les vagues contraires de la vie. Le théâtre a effectivement beaucoup de rapports avec la mer, rapports qui, à mon avis, sont basés sur l'idée de voir la première galerie, c'est-à-dire l'étage de l'entrée à partir de la Rambla, en tant que surface de la mer. La voûte de l'orchestre serait selon cette thèse la surface de l'eau regardée de dessous l'eau.

Quand l'eau se brise sur les rochers, elle se cabre et moutonne; c'est précisément ce que semble exprimer la balustrade de la première galerie.

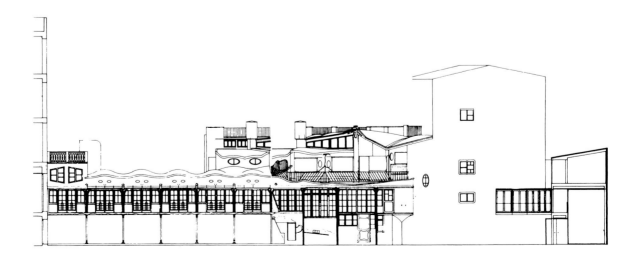

Unter dem Meerespiegel: Decken im Theater des
Arbeiterpatronats /
Below sea level: ceilings in the theatre of the
workers' patronage /
Au-dessous du niveau de la mer: plafonds du
théâtre du patronat ouvrier

An den ins Parkett hinabführenden Treppen — was nach unserer Hypothese bedeutet, ins Meer hinabzusteigen — sieht man Fische und kleine Rochen, wie jene, die sich am Strand in den Sand eingraben. Sind die Handläufe der zum zweiten Rang führenden Geländer gigantische Nähnadeln, mit denen Fischernetze ausgebessert werden?

Beside the steps leading down to the Stalls — or rather, according to our hypothesis, descending into the depths of the sea — there are fishes and small skate, the type that bury themselves in the sand on the beach. The handrails of the banisters leading up to the Upper Circle are gigantic sewing needles . . . for mending fishing nets?

Sur les escaliers qui descendent dans l'orchestre — ce qui signifie selon notre hypothèse descendre dans la mer —, on voit des poissons et de petites raies comme celles qui se terrent sous le sable de la plage. Les mains courantes des rampes qui mènent à la seconde galerie sont des aiguilles à coudre géantes . . . avec lesquelles on raccommode les filets de pêcheurs?

TORRE DE SAN SALVADOR

Einfamilienhaus / Detached house / Maison individuelle
Passeig de la Mare de Déu del Coll, Barcelona, 1909–1915

Von dem Haus, das Jujol für den Bauherrn Dr. San Salvador entworfen hat, sind nur die Gärten, die Mauern um das Grundstück und das Hausmeisterhäuschen fertiggestellt worden. Als man 1915 im Garten des Hauses eine Mineralquelle entdeckte, errichtete die Firma Aguas Radial, die ebenfalls Dr. San Salvador gehörte, dort eine Abfüllfabrik. Das Ganze befindet sich heute aufgrund jahrelanger Vernachlässigung in einem halbverfallenen Zustand.

All that survives of the house which Jujol designed for Dr. San Salvador is the garden, the boundary wall and the caretaker's cottage. Following the discovery of a mineral spring in the garden in 1915, the Aguas Radial company, which Dr. San Salvador also owned, built a bottling factory on the site. Due to years of neglect, the complex is today in a state of serious disrepair.

De la maison conçue par Jujol pour son client, le Dr. San Salvador, seuls les jardins, l'enceinte du terrain et la maisonnette du concierge ont été achevés. Lorsqu'on découvrit une source d'eau minérale dans le jardin en 1915, la firme Aguas Radial, qui appartenait également au Dr. San Salvador, érigea à cet endroit une usine de mise en bouteilles. L'ensemble est aujourd'hui à moitié délabré à cause d'une longue négligence.

$\dfrac{1}{100}$

CASA MAÑACH

Laden für Geldschränke und Eisenwaren / Shop for safes and hardware goods /
Magasin de coffres-forts et quincaillerie
Carrer de Ferran 57, Barcelona, 1911

Die Casa Mañach war ein Laden für Geldschränke und Eisenwaren in der Altstadt von Barcelona, der jetzt nicht mehr existiert. Das Innere sollte nach Jujols Worten »mit klingenden Algen und krachenden Feuerwerkskörpern« ausgeführt werden, und fügt man diesem Bild ein anderes, von der Familie erdachtes hinzu – das Bild des von der Wasseroberfläche aus gesehenen Meeresgrundes – und füllt die Innenräume mit Geldschränken und phantastischen, nach religiösen Motiven geformten Möbeln, dann wird aus dieser Arbeit eine der eindeutigsten, unbändigsten und inspiriertesten im gesamten Wirken Jujols.

The Casa Mañach was a shop, since destroyed, which sold safes and hardware goods in the historical heart of Barcelona. Its interior was to be executed, in Jujol's own words, »with tinkling algae and crackling fireworks«; if we add to this metaphor another proposed by the family – that of the sea floor seen from the water's surface –, and fill the rooms with strong-boxes and fantastic items of furniture modelled after religious motifs, then the work becomes one of the most unequivocal, unbridled and inspired of Jujol's entire œuvre.

La Casa Mañach était un magasin de coffres-forts et de quincaillerie de la vieille ville de Barcelone et n'existe plus aujourd'hui. L'intérieur devait être réalisé selon Jujol »avec des algues sonnantes et des pièces d'artifice claquantes«, et si l'on y ajoute une autre image inventée par la famille – l'image du fond de la mer vu à partir de la surface de l'eau – et que l'on remplit l'intérieur de coffres-forts et de meubles fantastiques façonnés d'après des motifs religieux, ce travail devient l'un des plus évidents, des plus pétulants et des plus inspirés de toute l'œuvre de Jujol.

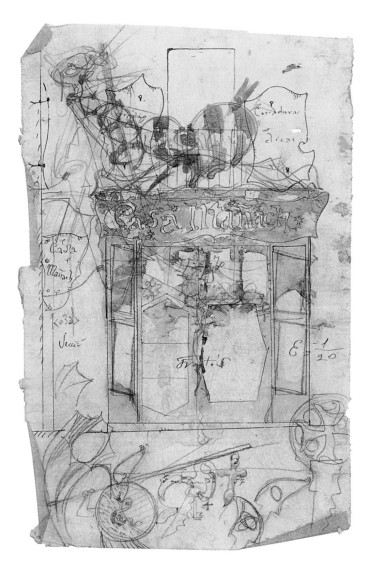

Türgriff der Casa Mañach / Doorknob of the Casa
Mañach / Poignée de porte de la Casa Mañach

Wie eine überdimensional große Gru-
benlampe fährt dieser Aufzug, den Jujol
für das Vestibül der Casa Iglésias entwarf,
zwischen den Treppen auf und ab.

The lift, planted by Jujol in the stairwell
of the Casa Iglésias, rides up and down
like a giant miner's lamp.

Cet ascenseur, conçu par Jujol pour le
vestibule de la Casa Iglésias, monte et
descend entre les escaliers comme un
grosse lampe de mineur.

PARROQUIA DE CONSTANTI

Ausführung von Innenarbeiten in der Pfarrkirche / Interior features of the parish church /
Travaux intérieurs de l'église paroissiale
Constantí, Tarragona, 1913

Für die Pfarrkirche von Constantí realisierte Jujol Innenarbeiten wie das Taufbecken, die Rückwand des Chorgestühls, verschiedene Möbelstücke – Bänke, Bet- und Beichtstühle – und ein paar Teile aus Schmiedeeisen, von denen die Skulptur eines Lamms hervorzuheben ist, das aus gefalzten und geschweißten Eisenblechstücken gefertigt wurde. Eigentlich recht unüblich für seine Arbeiten, standen für diese ausreichende finanzielle Mittel zur Verfügung. Dennoch konnte er sein Werk nicht zu Ende führen, was wiederum recht häufig geschah, weil der auftraggebende Pfarrherr verstarb.

Jujol was responsible for a number of interior features in Constantí parish church, including the font, the rear wall of the choir stall, various furnishings – pews, praying desks and confessionals – and a few wrought-iron pieces, of which the sculpture of a lamb, composed of folded and welded pieces of sheet iron, deserves particular attention. Rather unusually in Jujol's experience, there were adequate funds available to pay for these projects. He was nevertheless unable – as, by contrast, so often the case – to complete the commission, since the clergyman employing him died.

Pour l'église paroissiale de Constantí, Jujol a réalisé des travaux intérieurs tels que les fonts baptismaux, la paroi arrière des stalles, divers meubles – bancs, prie-Dieu et confessionnaux – et quelques pièces en fer forgé, parmi lesquelles on soulignera la sculpture d'un agneau fait de morceaux de tôle de fer repliés et soudés. Ces travaux sont à vrai dire fort inhabituels, car Jujol disposait de moyens financiers suffisants. Pourtant, il ne put terminer son œuvre – ce qui, par contre, arriva fréquemment – par suite du décès du curé qui lui avait passé la commande.

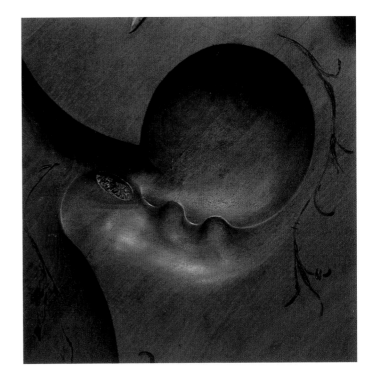

Metallarbeiten für die Pfarrkirche von Constantí /
Metalwork for the parish church of Constantí /
Travaux sur métal pour l'église paroissiale de
Constantí

TORRE DE LA CREU

Neubau eines Doppelhauses / Semi-detached house / Maison jumelée
Sant Joan Despí, Barcelona, 1913–1916

Der Torre de la Creu ist neben der Kirche von Vistabella und einigen kleineren Arbeiten einer der wenigen Neubauten, die Jujol ausgeführt hat. Das Haus wurde von seiner Tante Josefa Romeu in Auftrag gegeben und bestand ursprünglich aus zwei getrennten Wohnungen auf der Grundlage von fünf Zylindern unterschiedlicher Größe, von denen die beiden kleinsten die Treppenaufgänge der beiden Einheiten aufnahmen.

Jujols Bezüge zur organischen Welt und zur Tierwelt kommen hier am deutlichsten zum Ausdruck: Der Grundriß erinnert an eine Maus mit Kopf und Schwanz und eingezogenen Beinen.

Eine solche Form kann man sich unter Bäumen vorstellen, am Meer, am Rande einer Schlucht, freistehend oder in einer Gruppe mit anderen, paarweise oder in größerer Gemeinschaft, ganz nach Art dieses Tierchens, das der Anlage als Vorbild gedient haben könnte.

Das Haus hat einige Änderungen erfahren. Anfänglich für zwei getrennte Wohnungen konzipiert, wurde es 1966 zu einer einzigen Wohneinheit umgebaut, und die bizarre Dachbeschichtung aus hochkant gestellten Glasstücken – zusammengesuchtes Bruchgut von einer nahegelegenen Fabrik – durch eine glatte Auflage aus kleinen Keramikteilchen, dem sogenannten »gresite«, ersetzt. Das ganze Anwesen wirkt jetzt wie gefangen unter dem kitschigen Glanz dieses neuen Überzugs.

Derzeit dient der Torre de la Creu als Tageszentrum für geistig Behinderte. Die Innenräume des Hauses befinden sich in einem sehr guten Zustand, unpassend sind allein die nachträglich eingefügten Glasbausteinfenster des Treppenhauses und die geschmacklosen, ebenfalls später hinzugekommenen Treppenbeläge.

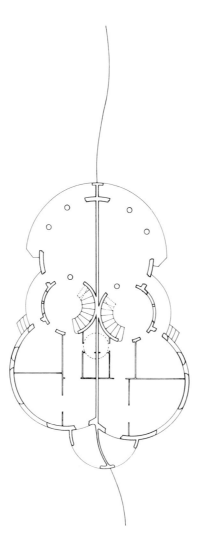

The Torre de la Creu, together with the church in Vistabella and a number of smaller commissions, represents one of the few new buildings which Jujol was to execute. It was commissioned by his aunt Josefa Romeu, and originally consisted of two separate apartments on a ground plan of five intersecting cylinders of varying sizes, of which the two smallest housed the steps leading up to the two apartments.

Jujol's ties with the organic world and animal kingdom here find their clearest expression: the plan recalls the form of a mouse, with a head, a tail and legs tucked in. The same form can be imagined standing beneath the trees, by the sea, on the edge of a ravine, alone or in a group, in pairs or with others, just like the animal which might have served it as model.

The house has undergone a number of modifications. Initially conceived as two separate apartments, it was converted in 1966 into a single living unit. Its bizarre roofing of protuding glass fragments – breakages salvaged from a nearby factory – was thereby replaced by a smooth layer of »gresite«, small pieces of ceramic. The house now appears as if trapped beneath the kitschy lustre of this new covering. The Torre de la Creu today serves as a day centre for the mentally handicapped. The rooms inside are still in very good condition; only the glass-brick windows of the stairwell and the tasteless stair covering, both added at a later date, are out of place.

La Torre de la Creu est, à côté de l'église de Vistabella et de quelques travaux de moindre importance, l'un des rares nouveaux bâtiments réalisés par Jujol. La maison lui fut commandée par sa tante Josefa Romeu et était composée à l'origine de deux appartements séparés reposant sur cinq cylindres de différentes grosseurs, les deux plus petits abritant les escaliers des deux unités.

Ici, les rapports de Jujol avec le monde organique et le monde animal sont exprimés très nettement. Le plan rappelle une souris avec une tête et une queue et des jambes rentrées. On peut imaginer une telle forme sous des arbres, au bord de la mer, au bord d'un précipice, solitaire ou dans un groupe avec d'autres, par groupe de deux ou plus, absolument à la manière de ce petit animal qui pourrait avoir servi de modèle à l'installation. La maison a subi quelques modifications. Initialement conçue pour deux appartements séparés, elle a été transformée en 1966 en une seule unité de logement, et le toit bizarre fait de petits morceaux de verre mis sur chant – fragments ramassés dans une usine proche – a été remplacé par une couche de petits morceaux de céramique, le dit »gresite«. La maison semble maintenant prisonnière sous l'éclat kitsch de cette nouvelle couche. Actuellement, la Torre de la Creu sert de centre à la journée pour handicapés mentaux. L'intérieur de la maison est en excellent état, seules les fenêtres en briques de verre de l'escalier ultérieurement rajoutées et les sols de mauvais goût également rajoutés sont déplacés.

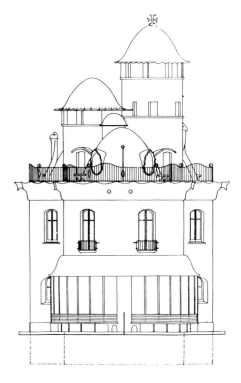

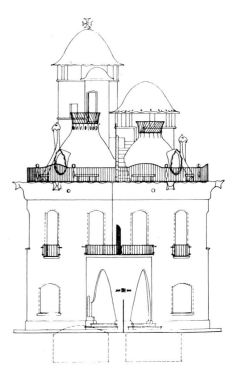

Das schmiedeeiserne Kreuz auf der höchsten Kuppel des Gebäudes hat dem Torre de la Creu seinen Namen gegeben. Man kennt ihn in Sant Joan Despí – wegen der Ähnlichkeit der Dächer mit einer Gruppe von fünf Eiern – auch als Torre dels Ous, aber auch mit Pilzen ist die Dachkonstruktion schon verglichen worden.

The wrought-iron cross on the tallest dome of the building gave the Torre de la Creu its name. In Sant Joan Despí, however, it is also known as Torre dels Ous, thanks to the similarity between its roofs and a batch of five eggs; others again have compared them to mushrooms.

La croix en fer forgé placée sur la plus haute coupole du bâtiment a donné son nom à la Torre de la Creu. Mais on la connaît également à Sant Joan Despí sous le nom de Torre dels Ous, parce que les toits ressemblent à un groupe de cinq œufs, mais ils ont aussi été comparés à des champignons.

Details der Dachlandschaft / Details of the rooftop
landscape / Détails des toitures

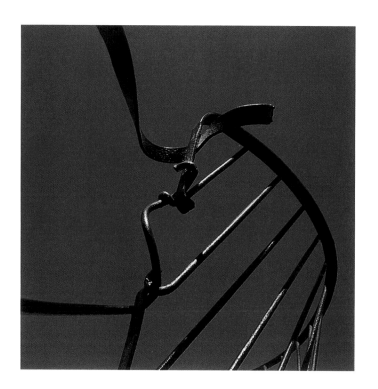

Es wird berichtet, daß Jujol auf dem Heimweg stets Dinge aufsammelte, die er auf der Straße fand, und an denen er zu Hause herumschnitzte, die er bearbeitete und zusammenfügte, bis er aus nutzlosem Material einen Rahmen, einen Sockel oder einen Schemel gemacht hatte. Er hatte es offenbar darauf angelegt, die Dinge unablässig in ihr Gegenteil zu verkehren. In ihrer ungestalten Form nahm er sie als Abfall, hauchte ihnen Leben ein und machte aus ihnen wieder nützliche, brauchbare Gegenstände. Dann wiederum tastete er sich an die ungestalte Form heran, bis die spezifischen Eigenheiten des Materials hervortraten, bei den Möbeln beispielsweise die faserige Struktur des Holzes; oder im Extrem: geometrische Formen, Inschriften, Symbole.

Während der Arbeiten am Bau des Torre de la Creu bringt der Schmied ein Gitter aus parallel laufenden, senkrechten Eisenstäben, von dem Jujol ihm zuvor einen Entwurf gezeichnet hat. Als er es auf der Baustelle entgegennimmt, beginnt er zusammen mit dem Schmied die Verwandlungsarbeit. Eigentlich ist es das Gegenteil von Arbeit, da es jetzt darum geht zu entspannen, dem Gitter alles zu nehmen, was nach Mühsal und ernsthafter, harter Arbeit aussieht; um – wie Heinrich Tessenow es ausdrückt – eine Art gezwungenes Lächeln in das Material hineinzubringen: Schläge, Beulen, Wülste, Einschnitte, Kerben, Verzerrungen. Tote Geometrie wird belebt, bis aus ihr lebendiges, federndes Material geworden ist.

Ein steter Drang also in zwei Richtungen auf dasselbe Ziel zu: einerseits Zerstörtes zu regenerieren und etwa aus nutzlosem, zerbrochenem Geschirr eine Dachbedeckung zu machen, andererseits ein Konstrukt zu zerlegen, Sprache aufzulösen und aus einem gewöhnlichen Satz – »Deu hi sia« – eine aufschäumende Gipsmörtelsoße zu machen. Betrachtet man Jujols Werk auf diese Weise, dann wird das Lager des Lumpensammlers zu einer Feste des Chaos. Der Urheber steht jedem Ordnungswillen gleichgültig gegenüber, allein darauf bedacht, das Außergewöhnliche dieser Welt hervorzuheben, die für ihn nur eine Vorstufe des Paradieses ist.

It is reported that Jujol, on his way home, would always stop to pick up things he found on the street; these he would later trim, rework and put back together until he had transformed the waste material into a frame, a plinth or a stool. He was clearly constantly out to transform objects into their opposite. He selected them in their unshaped form as waste, breathed life into them and made of them objects that were once again useful and practical. At the same time, however, he would also feel his way back towards the unshaped form, until the specific properties of the material came to the fore: the fibrous nature of wood in his furniture, or in extreme cases, geometric forms, inscriptions and symbols.

During construction work on the Torre de la Creu, the metal-worker brought along a railing composed of parallel vertical iron bars which he had manufactured to a design drawn beforehand by Jujol. Having taken delivery of it on site, Jujol – together with the metal-worker – immediately set about its transformation. The transformation process is really the opposite of the work process, since it is a matter of relaxing, of ridding the railings of everything that speaks of weary toil and strenuous labour, in order – as Heinrich Tessenow expressed it – to give the material a sort of forced smile: blows, dents, bulges, cuts, scars, distortions. Dead geometry is re-animated into living, pliant material.

A continual striving in two directions, therefore, towards the same goal: on the one hand, to regenerate the destroyed, to make roofing out of useless, broken tableware, and on the other to dismantle a construct, to disband language, to make a foaming stucco sauce out of the conventional phrase »Deu hi sia«. If we view Jujol's work in this light, the rag-and-boneman's storehouse becomes a celebration of chaos. The creator is indifferent to all will to order, his sole concern being to illuminate the dimension of the extraordinary in this world, which for him is simply a preliminary stage of paradise.

On raconte qu'en rentrant chez lui, Josep Maria Jujol ramassait toujours les choses qu'il trouvait dans la rue et les taillait à la maison, les façonnait et les assemblait, jusqu'à ce qu'il ait fait un cadre, un socle ou un escabeau à partir de matériaux inutiles. Il s'était apparemment donné pour but de changer sans cesse les choses en leur contraire. Sous leur aspect informe, il les prenait comme déchets, leur insufflait la vie et en faisait de nouveau des objets utiles et utilisables. Ensuite, par contre, il s'approchait de la forme ébauchée jusqu'à ce que ressortent les propriétés spécifiques des matériaux, pour les meubles par exemple la nature fibreuse du bois; ou à l'extrême: formes géométriques, inscriptions, symboles.

Pendant les travaux de construction de la Torre de la Creu, le forgeron apporte une grille faite de barreaux de fer parallèles et verticaux dont Jujol lui avait dessiné un plan auparavant. Quand il la reçoit sur le chantier, il commence avec le forgeron le travail de transformation. En réalité, c'est le contraire du travail, puisqu'il s'agit là de détendre, de prendre à la grille tout ce qui ressemble à de la fatigue et à du travail dur et sérieux; pour – comme le dit Heinrich Tessenow – mettre dans la matière une sorte de sourire contraint: coups, bosses, bourrelets, entailles, encoches, déformations. La géométrie morte est animée jusqu'à ce qu'elle se transforme en matière vivante et souple.

Un besoin constant donc dans deux directions vers un même but: d'une part, régénérer ce qui est détruit et peut-être faire une toiture avec de la vaisselle inutile, cassée, d'autre part, démonter une construction, décomposer une langue et faire un mortier de plâtre avec une phrase simple »Deu hi sia«. Si l'on considère l'œuvre de Jujol de cette façon, le dépôt du chiffonnier se transforme en citadelle du chaos. Le créateur fait face à tout désir d'ordre avec indifférence, uniquement soucieux de faire ressortir l'extraordinaire de ce monde qui n'est pour lui qu'un stade préliminaire du paradis.

Der Deckensturz des Treppenaufgangs
ist knorpelig wie ein Schlund. Bei nähe-
rem Hinsehen sind im Stuck die Worte
»Deu hi sia« zu erkennen.

The banisters run, cartilaginous like a
throat, into the ceiling, where, upon
close examination, the words »Deu hi
sia« can be read in the plaster.

Le linteau de la cage d'escalier est si-
nueux comme une gorge. En y regardant
de plus près, on peut reconnaître dans le
stuc les mots »Deu hi sia«.

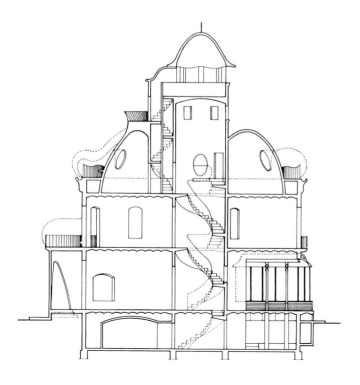

Treppenaufgang / Stairway / Montée d'escalier

Die früheren Speisezimmer / The former dining
rooms / Les anciennes salles à manger

Originalplan des ersten Stocks / Original plan of
the first floor / Plan original du premier étage

Metallsäulen im ehemaligen Speisezimmer / Metal
columns in what was formerly the dining room /
Colonnes métalliques dans l'ancienne salle à manger

TALLERS MAÑACH

Neubau einer Fabrikhalle / Construction of a new factory wing / Construction d'un
nouveau bâtiment d'usine
Carrer de la Riera de Sant Miquel 39, Barcelona, 1916–1918

Jujol plante für den Eigentümer des Geschäftshauses in der Carrer de Ferran – ein avantgardistischer Industrieller und der erste Händler der Kunst von Pablo Picasso – auch einen Fabrikflügel. Das Sheddach wurde mit Hilfe von Spannbögen errichtet und erinnert ebenso wie ein Teil des Innenraums im Torre de la Creu an das Innere eines riesigen Tieres. Als Strebepfeiler wurden an beiden Enden große Backsteinsäulen hochgezogen, die in ihrer Form den Zuhaltungen von Schlössern nachempfunden waren, denn das waren die wichtigsten Teile, die in dem hier untergebrachten Schlosserbetrieb hergestellt wurden.

Jujol also planned a factory wing for Mañach, the owner of the shop in the Carrer de Ferran (an avant-garde industrialist and Pablo Picasso's first dealer). Its shed roof was built with the aid of bracing arches and recalls, like part of the interior of the Torre de la Creu, the inside of a huge animal. The large brick pillars erected as buttresses at both ends were inspired by the shape of lock tumblers, the most important parts being manufactured in the locksmith's workshops which the building housed.

Jujol a également projeté un bâtiment d'usine pour le propriétaire du magasin de la Carrer de Ferran – un industriel avantgardiste et le premier marchand de Pablo Picasso. Le toit en redents a été construit à l'aide d'arcs de serrage et rappelle, comme une partie de l'intérieur de la Torre de la Creu, l'intérieur d'un animal géant. De grandes colonnes de brique ont été montées aux deux extrémités pour servir d'étais dont la forme rappelait les gâchettes de serrures, car c'étaient les pièces les plus importantes qui étaient fabriquées dans la serrurerie abritée sous ces voûtes.

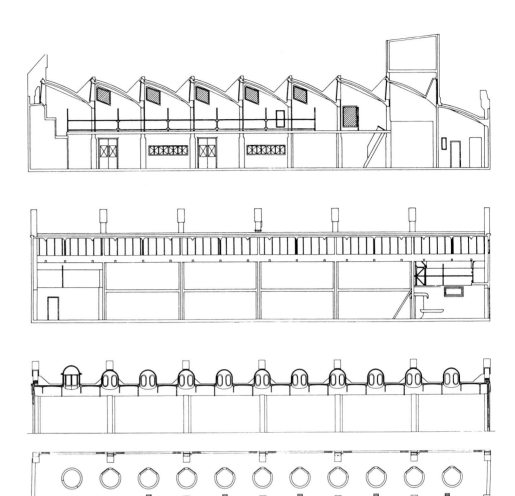

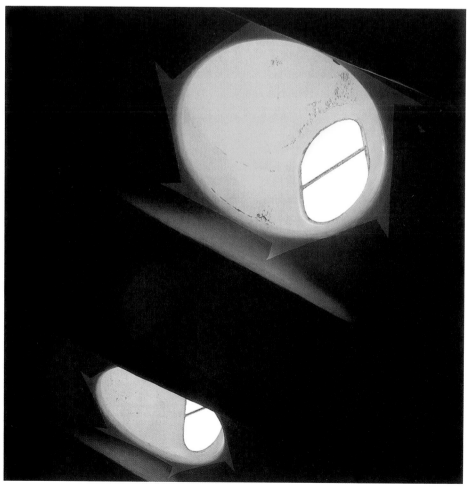

Licht bekamen die Werkräume durch Lichtschächte in Form von überdimensionalen Taucherhelmen. Strebepfeiler und Lichtschächte bilden eine ungewöhnliche Dachlandschaft, die die eigentliche Fassade dieses im Innenhof eines Gebäudekomplexes gelegenen Bauwerks ist.

Lighting was supplied from above via light shafts in the shape of outsized diving helmets. Buttresses and shafts together create an unusual roof landscape, the true façade of the building, which lies in the inner courtyard of a larger complex.

Les ateliers recevaient de la lumière grâce à des puits au jour en forme de casques de plongée surdimensionnés. Les étais et les puits au jour forment un extraordinaire paysage de toits qui constitue la façade proprement dite de cet édifice situé dans la cour intérieure d'un complexe de bâtiments.

Auf dem früheren Fabrikgelände wurde 1987 die
Escuela pública Josep Maria Jujol fertiggestellt;
Architekten: Jaume Bach und Gabriel Mora. Die
ehemalige Werkhalle dient jetzt als Schulhof.

The Escuela pública Josep Maria Jujol was completed at the former factory site in 1987; architects: Jaume Bach and Gabriel Mora. The original
workshop area now serves as a schoolyard.

L'Escuela pública Josep Maria Jujol fut achevée en
1987 sur l'ancien terrain d'usine; architectes:
Jaume Bach et Gabriel Mora. L'ancien atelier de
fabrication sert maintenant de préau.

CASA NEGRE

Umbau eines Gutshauses / Alterations to a manor-house /
Transformation d'un domaine
Sant Joan Despí, Barcelona, 1915–1926

Irgendein Haus: Fenster, Wände, Fußböden sind Elemente oder Materialien ohne Leben, und die Luft in ihnen ist so unbedeutend wie die in den Straßen der Stadt oder draußen vor der Tür. Diese Luft jedoch, dieselbe Luft, die man überall atmet, kann sich für einen gläubigen Menschen radikal verändern, wenn über der Eingangstür oder an den Wänden der Diele ein religiöses Bild, ein Heiliges Herz oder die Jungfrau von Montserrat hängt. Von diesem Moment an umschließt das, was seelenloses Konstrukt war, geweihte Luft, der Raum hat eine Bedeutung, die Behausung ist ein Haus. Auf diese – zugegebenermaßen etwas parteiische – Art könnte man Architektur interpretieren: Konstruktion plus himmlischer Segen ist Architektur.

Die wichtigsten Arbeiten an der Casa Negre waren die Neugestaltungen der Fassade und des Treppenhauses, die meiner Meinung nach direkter Ausdruck jenes Architekturverständnisses sind, das ich vorhin erwähnte. Wenn die Schöpfung jenes Heiligenbildes, das für einen frommen Menschen aus der Konstruktion Architektur macht, einem Architekten überlassen ist, der über das ganze Haus verfügt, um seiner Frömmigkeit Ausdruck zu verleihen, und wenn dieser Architekt der Auffassung ist, sein Werk müsse Zeugnis von Gott ablegen, was für Jujol ohne Zweifel zutrifft – dann wird der Malgrund der Fassade zu einem Sendbrief des himmlischen Reiches. Um das Altarbild der Heiligen Jungfrau geschart, das nach Jujols Entwurf in das obere Mittelfenster der Empore eingraviert war, zeigt dieser Malgrund Girlanden, Medaillons und Inschriften, die den Ruhm Mariens verkünden: Das Symbol, die Abstraktion, ist Gegenstand geworden.

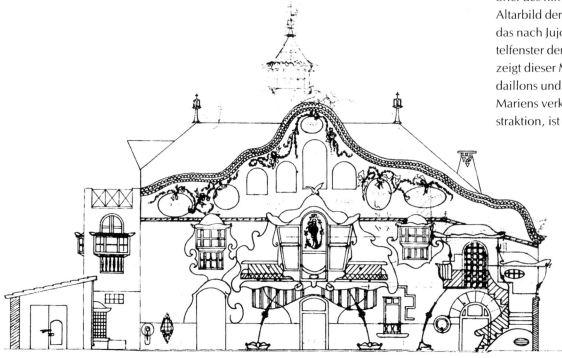

Imagine a typical house: the windows, walls and floors will be elements and materials without life, and the air within them will carry no more significance than the air in the city streets or outside the front door. For a believer, however, this air – the same air as is breathed everywhere – can take on a radically new meaning should a religious icon, a Sacred Heart or a Blessed Virgin of Montserrat, hang above the entrance or on the hallway walls. From that moment onwards, what was previously a soulless construct now encompasses sacred air; space has meaning, housing becomes a house. Architecture itself might be interpreted in a similar, admittedly rather one-sided way – as construction plus heavenly blessing.

Jujol's most important contributions to the Casa Negre were the redesign of the façade and the stairwell, both of which, in my opinion, directly voice the interpretation of architecture suggested above. Just as the presence of a religious painting may transform construction into architecture in the eyes of the pious, so – if that pious person is an architect (and hence has at his disposal an entire house with which to express his faith), and one who believes his work should bear witness to God, as Josep Maria Jujol clearly does – an entire façade may become the pictorial ground for an epistle from Heaven. In the Casa Negre, this ground bears garlands, roundels and inscriptions in praise of Mary, grouped around the altarpiece of the Virgin Mary which was engraved into the top half of the central balcony of the window to a design by Jujol. Symbol and abstraction have become objects.

Une maison quelconque: les fenêtres, les murs, les sols sont des éléments ou des matériaux sans vie, et l'air qu'ils contiennent est aussi peu important que celui qui se trouve dans les rues de la ville ou dehors, devant la porte. Cet air, toutefois, le même air que l'on respire partout, peut se modifier radicalement pour un croyant quand une image religieuse, un Sacré-Cœur ou une Vierge de Montserrat est accroché au-dessus de la porte d'entrée ou au mur du vestibule. A partir de là, ce qui était une construction sans âme renferme de l'air sacré, la pièce a un sens, le logement est une maison. De cette manière – un peu incomplète, il faut l'admettre –, on pourrait interpréter l'architecture: construction plus bénédiction divine égale architecture.

Les travaux les plus importants effectués dans la Casa Negre ont été la recréation de la façade et de l'escalier qui sont à mon avis l'expression directe de compréhension de l'architecture évoquée plus haut. L'image sainte qui, pour un homme pieux, fait de la construction une architecture, peut acquérir une signification qui – si cet homme est architecte et dispose donc de toute la maison pour exprimer sa piété et pense que son œuvre doit rendre témoignage à Dieu, et c'est sans aucun doute le cas de Josep Maria Jujol – transforme le fond de la façade en lettre ouverte du royaume des cieux. Groupé autour du tableau d'autel de la sainte Vierge, qui était gravé dans la fenêtre médiane supérieure de la galerie d'après les plans de Jujol, ce fond présente des guirlandes, des médaillons et des inscriptions à la gloire de Marie: le symbole, l'abstraction, est devenu objet.

Die Hauptfassade vor und nach dem Umbau /
The main façade before and after the renovation /
Façade principale avant et après les transformations

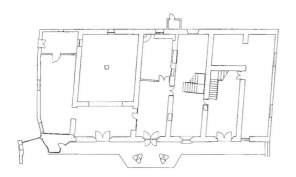 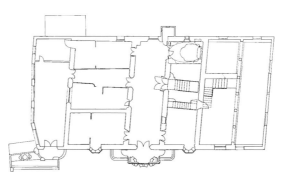

Die Casa Negre war früher ein Gutshaus, in dem Jujol auf Bitten der Familie Negre von 1914 bis 1926 Um- und Ausbauten vornahm, denen er ähnlich viel Zeit und Aufmerksamkeit widmete wie den Arbeiten an der Casa Bofarull. Und in der Tat: Zeigt die Casa Bofarull am markantesten auf, wie wichtig das Umland von Tarragona für Jujols Werk war, so hat die Casa Negre eine vergleichbare Bedeutung in bezug auf religiöse Darstellungskunst und Volksbrauchtum.

The Casa Negre was formerly a large manor-house to which, at the request of the Negre family, Jujol made extensive alterations between 1914 and 1926. He thus devoted a similar amount of time and attention to his work here as to the Casa Bofarull. And whereas the Casa Bofarull most strikingly illustrates the importance of the Tarragona countryside for Jujol's work, a role of comparable significance is taken in the Casa Negre by religious representational art and popular customs.

La Casa Negre était autrefois une maison domaniale dans laquelle Jujol entreprit à la demande de la famille Negre des transformations et des aménagements entre 1914 et 1926, leur consacrant autant de temps et d'attention qu'aux travaux de la Casa Bofarull. Effectivement: alors que la Casa Bofarull montre très clairement combien les alentours de Tarragone étaient importants pour l'œuvre de Jujol, la Casa Negre a une signification parallèle pour ce qui est de l'art de la représentation religieuse et des usages populaires.

Man muß sich das Haus umgeben von Feldern und Pflanzungen vorstellen, wie es zur Zeit der Umbauarbeiten wohl ausgesehen hat. Vor dem Haupteingang befand sich damals der Garten, von dem, als diese Aufnahmen entstanden, nur noch ein paar Bäume und die skurrilen Rippen eines gewölbten Laubengangs übriggeblieben waren. Im Zuge einer Neugestaltung der Plaça de Catalunya sind auch diese letzten Versatzstücke eines ehemals ländlichen Umfeldes verschwunden: Heute liegt die rückwärtige Fassade der Casa Negre an der Zufahrt zu einer Tiefgarage.

The house should be visualized within a setting of fields and plantations, as it must have looked at the time of its renovation. In front of the main entrance lay the garden, of which – at the time these photographs were taken – a few trees and the skeletal ribs of an arched pergola still survived. Even the last testaments to a once rural environment were removed in the course of the redesign of the Plaça de Catalunya; the rear facade of the Casa Negre today lies beside the entrance to an underground car park.

Il faut imaginer la maison environnée de champs et de plantations, telle qu'elle était à l'époque des transformations. Devant l'entrée principale se trouvait alors le jardin dont il ne restait, lorsque ces vues ont été prises, que quelques arbres et les grotesques nervures d'arcades voûtées. Par suite de la transformation de la Plaça de Catalunya, ces dernières décorations d'un milieu autrefois champêtre ont également disparu; la façade arrière de la Casa Negre se trouve aujourd'hui à l'entrée d'un garage souterrain.

Die beiden Eisenstreben endeten in je einer Kunststeinbank in der Form von drei Reitsätteln. Durch die Erhöhung des Gehsteigs und jahrelange Nachlässigkeit blieben davon nur ein Paar Stümpfe übrig.
Das Gebinde aus Kreuz, Ähren und Weintrauben trug ehemals ein riesiger Vogel an einem Seiteneingang der Casa Negre im Schnabel.

Two artificial stone benches in the form of three riding saddles formerly stood one at each foot of the iron stanchions. Owing to the raising of the pavement and years of neglect, only a few stumps now remain.
A giant bird once carried in its beak this garland of a cross, ears of corn and grapes beside a side entrance to the Casa Negre.

Les deux étais en fer se terminaient chaque fois par un banc en pierre artificielle qui avait la forme de trois selles. A cause de l'élévation du trottoir et d'une négligence de plusieurs années, seuls les deux tronçons représentés sur la photographie sont restés.
L'ensemble fait d'une croix, d'un épi et d'une grappe de raisin, se trouvait autrefois dans le bec d'un oiseau géant placé à une entrée latérale de la Casa Negre.

Am Torre de la Creu verschwanden die geometrischen Linien der Gitter durch Deformation, hier durch Auflagen aus gebogenen, verbeulten und eingeschnittenen Eisenblechen. Es gab noch ein ebenso prachtvolles Gitter an der Casa Negre, von dem ich Photos gesehen habe: Bei ihm sind die beiden vertikalen Mittelstäbe herausgenommen und an ihrer Stelle Hacken und anderes landwirtschaftliches Arbeitsgerät eingesetzt und mit Hilfe der beiden herausgelösten Eisenstäbe mit dem restlichen Gitter verbunden worden.

In the Torre de la Creu, the geometric lines of the railings were banished by means of deformation; the same effect is achieved here with a garnish of sheet iron, which is dented, bent and torn instead. There is another, equally magnificent grille at the Casa Negre, of which I have seen photographs: its two vertical centre bars have been removed and replaced by hoes and other agricultural implements, which have then been secured to the rest of the railings with the aid of the two original bars.

A la Torre de la Creu, les lignes géométriques des grilles ont disparu à cause de la déformation; ici, on a posé des tôles de fer bosselées, tordues et déchirées. Il y avait encore à la Casa Negre une grille tout aussi magnifique dont j'ai vu des photos: les deux barreaux verticaux du milieu ont été enlevés et remplacés par des binettes et autres outils agricoles, et reliés au reste de la grille à l'aide des deux barreaux de fer détachés.

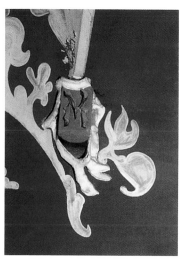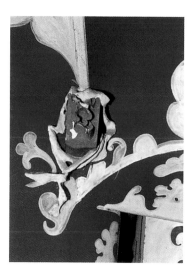

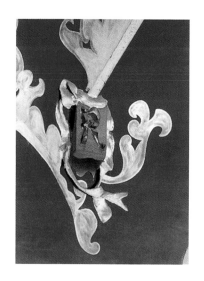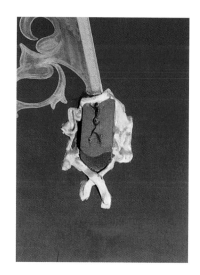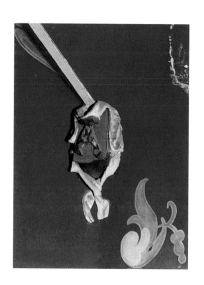

Die Buchstaben auf den acht Konsolen im Treppenhaus bilden die Worte »Ave Maria«. /
The letters on the eight consoles in the staircase
form the words »Ave Maria«. /
Les lettres appliquées sur les huit corbeaux de
l'escalier forment les mots »Ave Maria«.

Wirkt der Besuch der Heiligen Jungfrau
auf die Fassade wie »der Donnerschlag
des Vaters im Gewand einer Melodie«,
so ist es im Treppenhaus ein Engel, der
diesen Raum zu seinem Zimmer macht.
An seinen Schleiern befestigt, schwebt er
unter der Decke, schaut herab auf den
blaugoldenen Glanz einer Nacht weiß-
rauchender Fackeln und glühender
Lämpchen. Das Karussell dreht sich, die
Nacht ist ein Fest, auf dem der Engel fun-
kelnder Stern und Betrachter ist.
Jede Konsole besteht aus einem bemalten
Karton, auf dem ein aus Gipsbinden ge-
formter Buchstabe angebracht ist.

If the appearance of the Blessed Virgin on
the façade is like »the thunder of the
Father in the guise of a melody«, in the
stairwell it is an angel who claims the
room for his own. Attached by his veils,
he floats beneath the ceiling, looking
down on the blue-golden sparkle of a
night full of smoking torches and glowing
lamps. The merry-go-round is spinning,
the night is a carnival at which the angel
is a twinkling star and an observer.
Each console consists of a painted cardboard box bearing a letter shaped out of
plaster bandage.

Alors que l'apparition de la sainte Vierge
sur la façade fait l'effet d'un »coup de
tonnerre sous forme de mélodie«, un
ange fait de l'escalier son logement. At-
taché à ses voiles, il flotte sous le plafond, regarde en bas l'éclat bleu et or
d'une nuit de flambeaux fumants et de
petites lampes ardentes. Le manège
tourne, la nuit est une fête où l'ange est
étoile scintillante et spectateur. Chaque
corbeau est composé d'un carton peint
sur lequel est apposée une lettre faite
avec des bandes de plâtre.

Die von Jujol gestalteten Türen im ersten Stock führen zum großen Wohnraum, zum Kinderzimmer, zur Kapelle und zu Bibliothek bzw. Studierzimmer. Mit Ausnahme der Tür zur Kapelle sind alle Türen mit Feuergravuren und blauer Oberbemalung ausgeführt. Besonders ausgearbeitet sind die beiden Puppenköpfe, die – wie ich annehme – auf das Mädchenzimmer verweisen, und das auf dem Wellenkamm tanzende Buch, das die zum Studierzimmer führende Tür kennzeichnet.

The doors leading off the corridor on the first floor open onto the living room, the chapel and the library or study. Designed by Jujol, all except the door to the chapel are decorated with engravings and a scrolling upper surround of blue paint. Particularly detailed are the two dolls' heads which – I assume – indicate the girl's room, and the book dancing on the crest of a wave which marks the door leading onto the study.

Les portes du premier étage conçues par Jujol donnent sur la pièce principale, la chambre d'enfants, la chapelle et la bibliothèque ou cabinet de travail. A l'exception de la porte de la chapelle, toutes les portes sont pourvues de gravures au feu et de peinture bleue. Les deux têtes de poupée qui renvoient – comme je le suppose – à la chambre de jeune fille, et un livre dansant sur la crête des vagues qui caractérise la porte donnant sur le cabinet de travail sont particulièrement travaillés.

Auf dem winzigen Raum von schätzungsweise zwei mal drei Metern drängt sich die ganze Pracht einer barocken Kirche, und als wäre das noch nicht genug, baumelt von der Decke ein enormer Lüster aus einem Gespinst von Eisenbändern herab. Wie viele Elemente von festlichen Bräuchen, religiöser Formgebung und alter Tradition – Feiern, Feuer, Prozessionen etc. – in der Casa Negre ihre Darstellung auch finden, in der Kapelle werden sie allesamt untergebracht und zeigen sich selbstbewußt als historisches Modell eines religiösen Raums.

All the glory of a baroque church is here squeezed into a tiny space of approximately two by three metres. As if that were not enough, an enormous chandelier woven from strips of iron swings from the ceiling. The chapel brings together all the elements of festive custom, religious form and ancient tradition – ceremonies, fire, processions, etc. – portrayed throughout the Casa Negre, deliberately fusing them into the historical model of a religious room.

Dans la minuscule pièce d'à peu près deux mètres sur trois se presse toute la magnificence d'une église baroque, et comme si cela n'était pas encore suffisant, un énorme lustre fait d'un tissu de rubans de fer est suspendu au plafond. Les éléments de coutumes solennelles, de formes religieuses et d'anciennes traditions – fête, feu, processions, etc. – également représentés dans la Casa Negre ont tous une place dans la chapelle et se montrent conscients de leur valeur comme modèle historique de pièce sacrée.

CASA BOFARULL

Umbau eines Gutshauses / Alterations to a manor-house /
Transformation d'un domaine
Els Pallaresos, Tarragona, 1914–1931

Die Casa Bofarull ist das Bauwerk, an dem Jujol die längste Zeit arbeitete. Aber was noch wichtiger ist, ihm stand diese Zeit auch zur Verfügung: fünfzehn Jahre. Dennoch blieb das Haus unvollendet. Anscheinend bestand der Hauptteil seiner Anwesenheit darin, jeweils ein paar Tage im Haus zu wohnen und sich von den Schwestern Dolores und Pepita Bofarull bedienen und versorgen zu lassen. Ein Freund des Hauses erzählte mir lächelnd, er erinnere sich an Jujol, wie er einem Maurer, der einen Stein zurechtklopfte, Anweisungen gab: »Schlag' da noch etwas ab, die Kante noch, dort noch was«, bis der Stein in Stücke brach, und dann ging Jujol einfach davon. Sr. Maguerolas, der Sohn des Kunstschmieds, der zusammen mit Jujol an der Casa Bofarull gearbeitet hatte, erinnert sich, daß sein Vater beim Einsetzen des Treppengeländers an einem Eisenrohr bog, es knickte und drehte, wie Jujol es ihm anwies. Der junge Maguerolas erinnert sich auch, daß es öfter vorkam, daß ein Rohr brach und Jujol dann mit dem abgebrochenen Metallstück schimpfte, weil es sich vom Ganzen gelöst hatte. Jedenfalls hatte die grenzenlose Verfügbarkeit von Zeit sowie die unauflösliche Verschmelzung von Landleben und handwerklicher und künstlerischer Tätigkeit ein bis ins letzte Detail ausgefeiltes Bauwerk zum Ergebnis.

Die wesentlichen Eingriffe bestanden in dem Bau eines Portals, in der Neugestaltung der rückwärtigen Fassade, die auf die Felder ging, in der Verlängerung des Treppenhauses, das aus dem überdachten Gebäude herausgeführt wurde und zu dem mit dem Erzengel Gabriel gekrönten Aussichtsturm führte, die Gartenmauer und der Laubengang des Waschplatzes auf dem angrenzenden Grundstück. Weiterhin wurde eine Unzahl kleinerer Veränderungen vorgenommen, allesamt kunsthandwerklicher Art: schmiedeeiserne Arbeiten, Sgraffiti, Glasarbeiten, Mobiliar.

The Casa Bofarull is the building on which Jujol worked over the longest period of time. Even more significant, however, is the fact that he was allowed to take so long – fifteen years. Even then the house remained unfinished. It seems that his attendance consisted largely of his living in the house for a few days at a time and being waited upon by the Bofarull sisters, Dolores and Pepita. An acquaintance of the family smilingly told me how he remembered Jujol instructing a mason, who was chipping a stone into shape, to »knock a bit more off there, and off the edge, and a bit more off there« – until the stone shattered and Jujol departed the scene.

Sr. Maguerolas, son of the art metal-worker who worked with Jujol on the Casa Bofarull, remembers his father installing the banisters, bending and twisting the iron bars as Jujol directed him. The young Maguerolas also remembers that the bars would frequently snap; Jujol would then scold the broken piece of metal for detaching itself from the whole. At all events, the unlimited availability of time, and the indissoluble union of rural life and craftsmanly and artistic activity, resulted in a work of architecture polished in its every detail.

Jujol's most significant alterations included the building of a portal, the redesign of the rear façade facing the fields, the extension of the stairway which led out of the covered building and across to the viewing tower crowned by the Archangel Gabriel, and the building of the garden wall and the pergola in the laundry area on the neighbouring plot. He also made countless minor modifications, all of a handicraft nature: wrought-iron compositions, sgraffiti, works in glass, furnishings.

La Casa Bofarull est le bâtiment auquel Jujol a travaillé le plus longtemps. Mais ce qui est encore plus important, c'est qu'il a aussi eu ce temps à sa disposition: quinze ans. Pourtant, la maison est restée inachevée. Apparemment, la majeure partie de sa présence consistait à chaque fois à habiter quelques jours dans la maison et à se faire servir et entretenir par les sœurs Dolores et Pepita Bofarull. Un familier de la maison m'a raconté en souriant qu'il se souvenait comment Jujol avait un jour donné des instructions à un maçon en train de tailler une pierre. »Casse encore un peu là, encore cette arête, encore un peu là«, jusqu'à ce que la pierre se casse en morceaux, et alors Jujol était parti.

Sr. Maguerolas, le fils du ferronnier qui travaillait dans la Casa Bofarull, se souvient que son père avait aidé Jujol à placer la balustrade et avait courbé un tuyau de fer, l'avait coudé et tordu, comme le lui demandait Jujol. Le jeune Maguerolas se souvient également qu'il était fréquent qu'un tuyau se casse et que Jujol se mettait alors à invectiver le morceau de métal cassé parce qu'il s'était détaché du tout.

En tout cas, la disponibilité illimitée du temps, le mélange de vie champêtre et d'activité artisanale et artistique eurent pour conséquence une construction fignolée jusque dans le moindre détail.

Les principales interventions ont été la construction d'un portail, le remaniement de la façade arrière qui donnait sur les champs, le prolongement de l'escalier sortant du bâtiment couvert et menant à la tour panoramique couronnée de l'archange Gabriel, le mur du jardin et les arcades du lavoir sur le terrain avoisinant. En outre, un grand nombre de petites modifications ont été effectuées, toutes d'ordre artisanal: travaux de ferronnerie, sgraffites, travaux de verrerie, mobilier.

Der Engel war ursprünglich mit Flügeln und einer Drehachse versehen, so daß er als Wetterfahne funktionierte; das Geländer verfügt über zwei Ausleger in Form von Feuerschalen, in die Brennholz gelegt wurde. Man stelle sich den Engel vor, wie er sich in der abendlichen Brise dreht, wie er sich, beleuchtet vom sanften Licht der beiden Feuer, gegen den Abendhimmel abhebt, und man begreift, daß Jujol wieder die Vereinigung, das Zusammenspiel von Flur und Natur zelebriert, ohne diesmal auf Insekten, auf die Dünung der Felder oder des Meeres zurückzugreifen, wie er es mit dem Eisen und dem Sgraffito getan hat, sondern auf Elemente, die ebenfalls zur Landschaft von Tarragona gehören: den Wind und den strahlenden Himmel.

The angel was originally designed with wings and a pivot and functioned as a weather vane. From the railings project two brackets in the form of shallow bowls, in which firewood was once burned. Imagining the angel gently turning in the evening breeze, softly lit by the flickering flames of the two fires as it hovers against the evening sky, it becomes clear that Jujol is here celebrating the unification, the interplay of open farmland and nature, whereby he turns not to insects, not to the swell of the fields or the ocean as he did with iron and sgraffito, but to elements which are just as much part of the Tarragona landscape: the wind and the glorious skies.

A l'origine, l'ange était pourvu d'ailes et d'un axe de rotation, de sorte qu'il fonctionnait comme une girouette; la balustrade a deux bras en forme de braseros dans lesquels on mettait du bois de chauffage. Imaginons l'ange tournant dans la brise vespérale, se soulevant, illuminé par la douce lumière des deux feux, vers le ciel du soir, et l'on comprend que Jujol célèbre de nouveau l'union, l'harmonie de la campagne et de la nature, sans remonter cette fois aux insectes, à la houle dans les champs ou sur la mer, comme il l'a fait avec le fer et les sgraffites, mais aux éléments qui font aussi partie du paysage de Tarragone: le vent et le ciel radieux.

Himmel, Luft, oben der knirschend sich
drehende Engel und darunter auf der
Dachschräge Teller, Tassen, Flaschen,
ein Krug. Natur und Alltag vereint in Els
Pallaresos. Die Überreste eines hypothe-
tischen Frühstücks im Garten des Hauses
als Dachauflage, aus der sich der Krug
heraushebt und, als Weingefäß den
Weingärten zugewandt, auf das brüder-
liche Verhältnis zwischen dem Land und
den Bewohnern des Hauses verweist.

Sky, air, the angel overhead grating as he
turns, and on the hip of the lower roofing
section – plates, cups, bottles, a carafe.
Nature and daily life are fused in Els Pallaresos. The remains of a hypothetical
breakfast out in the garden become the
material for a roof, from which the carafe
– as the vessel of wine, facing the vineyards – stands out in clear relief,
emphasizing the fraternal relationship
between the house's inhabitants and
the land which surrounds them.

Le ciel, l'air, en haut l'ange qui tourne en
grinçant, et dessous, sur le plan du toit,
des assiettes, des tasses, des bouteilles,
une cruche. La nature et le quotidien
sont réunis à Els Pallaresos. Les restes
d'un hypothétique petit-déjeuner dans le
jardin de la maison comme toiture d'où
sort la cruche qui, tournée vers les vignes
comme récipient à vin, renvoie à la relation fraternelle entre le pays et les habitants de la maison.

Ein Schuppen voll unbrauchbarer landwirtschaftlicher Gerätschaften kommt für Jujol einem Baustofflager gleich. Wurde zuvor aus einem Haken ein Rüssel, wird jetzt aus einer Hacke ein Gitter oder ein Scharnier; wurde zuvor der Gegenstand oder sein Gebrauch von der Figur überlagert, so geschieht jetzt das Gegenteil, und er nimmt eine nutzlose Figur, um einen Nutzen für sie zu finden. Wie im Park Güell oder im Theater des Arbeiterpatronats ist alles Material, jeder Gegenstand eine Schöpfung des Herrn und daher kostbar.

For Jujol, a shed full of unwanted agricultural implements is tantamount to a treasurehouse of materials. But where a hook previously became a trunk, a hoe now becomes a railing or a hinge; where Jujol previously masked an object or its function behind a figure, he now does the opposite, and takes a useless figure in order to find a use for it. As in Park Güell and the Workers' Patronage theatre, everything is material, every object a creation of the Lord and precious.

Un hangar plein d'outillage agricole inutilisable équivaut pour Jujol à un entrepôt de matériaux de construction. Alors qu'un crochet se transformait précédemment en trompe, une binette se transforme maintenant en grille ou en charnière; alors que la figure se superposait précédemment à l'objet ou à son usage, c'est désormais le contraire, et il prend une figure inutile pour lui trouver une utilité. Comme dans le Parque Güell ou dans le Teatro del Patronato Obrero, tout est matériau, chaque objet est une création du Seigneur et donc précieux.

Für mich sind die Sgraffiti der Casa Bofarull die schönsten, die Jujol jemals gemacht hat. Obwohl sie im Lauf der Zeit Schaden genommen haben, sieht man ihnen noch die Stunden und Tage an, die auf ihre Herstellung verwendet worden sind. Eine Fensternische ist Ausgangspunkt einer Zeichnung, die ein eigenes Leben zu entwickeln beginnt und sich über die ganze Wand auszubreiten droht. Der auf die Wandoberfläche oder über ein Fenster gemalte Anfangsbuchstabe B für »Bofarull« entlädt sich zu einer von der Geometrie des Buchstabens ausgehenden Komposition von Linien und Eingebungen, die ihre Form in Vögeln, Sternen etc. finden.

The sgraffiti in the Casa Bofarull are, for me, the finest that Jujol ever produced. Although they have suffered over the course of time, they still reflect the hours and days that went into their making. A window recess is the starting-point for a drawing, which begins to take on its own life and threatens to spread over the entire wall. The initial B (for Bofarull), painted on the wall or over a window, discharges into a composition of lines and impulses derived from the geometry of the letter, which find their form in birds, stars, etc.

Pour moi, les sgraffites de la Casa Bofarull sont les plus beaux que Jujol ait jamais faits. Bien qu'ils aient subi des dommages avec le temps, on voit encore qu'il a fallu des journées entières pour les réaliser. Une niche vitrée est le point de départ d'un dessin qui commence à développer sa propre âme et menace de s'étendre sur tout le mur. L'initiale B de Bofarull peinte sur le mur ou au-dessus d'une fenêtre se décharge pour devenir une composition de lignes et d'inspirations partant de la géométrie de la lettre, qui trouvent leur forme dans des oiseaux, des étoiles, etc.

Der Laubengang, in dem die Feldsteine
als etwas Besonderes herausgestellt werden, ist eine pflanzenartige, an Weinran-
ken erinnernde Gewölbekonstruktion,
die dem Waschplatz Schatten spendete.

The pergola, in which fieldstones are
presented to us as something remarkable,
took the form of a plantlike, arched construction reminiscent of vine tendrils,
which provided the laundry area with
shade.

Les arcades, dans lesquelles les pierres
sont mises en évidence en tant que quelque chose de particulier sont une construction en voûte ressemblant à une
plante et rappelant les vrilles de la vigne
qui faisait de l'ombre au lavoir.

Noch schöner als der Laubengang ist vielleicht die Umfassungsmauer, in die Pflanzen und eine Bank eingelassen sind – eine Mauer, die sich krümmt und senkt und sich mit Spitzen und abrupt eingeschnittenen Linien gegen den Himmel abhebt: eine lebendige, von den umliegenden Feldern hervorgebrachte, merkwürdige Kreatur.

Dasselbe gilt für die Mauer, die den Garten des Hauses umschließt. Der Eindruck ihrer Lebendigkeit kulminiert in dem dreieckigen Fenster – einziger Durchblick zu den Feldern dahinter –, das sich über die Mauerkrone hinaushebt, als recke jemand den Kopf, um hinüberzuschauen.

Even more beautiful than the pergola, perhaps, is the boundary wall, in which plants and a bench are bedded, and which curves and undulates and reaches heavenwards in peaks and abruptly interrupted lines – a strange, living creature brought forth by the surrounding fields. The same is true of the wall which encircles the garden: its impression of being alive culminates in the triangular window – the only view through to the fields beyond – which rises above the crown of the wall like someone craning his head to see over the top.

Il y a peut-être encore plus beau que les arcades: le mur de pourtour, sur lequel poussent des plantes et où est placé un banc, se courbe, s'affaisse et se détache sur le ciel avec des pointes et des lignes gravées abruptement, vivant, curieuse créature engendrée par les champs alentour.

Il en va de même avec le mur enfermant le jardin de la maison: l'impression de vie culmine dans la fenêtre triangulaire – unique percée vers les champs, derrière – qui se soulève au-dessus du chaperon, comme si quelqu'un allongeait le cou pour regarder par-dessus.

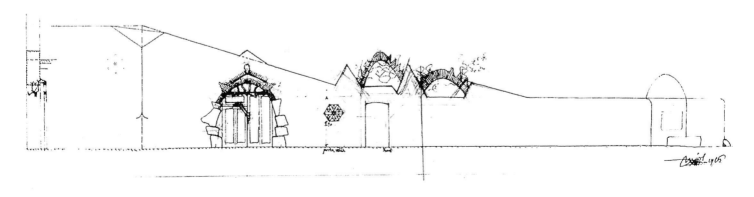

Träger, Flacheisen, Schindeln und Haken sind tote Gegenstände, die – ebenso wie die Mauern des Waschplatzes und vom Garten – so behandelt werden, daß sie im Zusammenspiel oder Einvernehmen von Natur und Landschaft mitwirken: Sie werden förmlich lebendig und verwandeln sich in Schnäbel, Hände, Rüssel oder Insekten.
Sprach ich oben von der Ummauerung des Waschplatzes als einer von den umliegenden Feldern hervorgebrachten merkwürdigen Kreatur, so gilt dies auch für den Wasserspeier des Brunnens im Garten, mit dem Unterschied, daß dieser aus Eisen ist. Er wölbt sich wie ein bukkelndes Geziefer. Glückliche Stunden des Architekten, des Kunstschmieds, der Schwestern Bofarull. Phantastisch!

Supports, flat bars, shingling and hooks are inanimate objects which – just like the walls surrounding the laundry area and garden – are treated in such a way as to become part of the interplay or harmony of nature and landscape: they come to life and transform themselves into beaks, hands, trunks and insects.
Just as I spoke of the wall surrounding the laundry area as a strange creature brought forth by the surrounding fields, so the same applies to the iron gargoyle in the garden's fountain, which arches over the rim like some curving reptile. Happy days for the architect, the metalworker, the Bofarull sisters. Fantastic.

Les poutres, les aciers plats, les bardeaux et les crochets sont des objets morts qui – tout comme les murs du lavoir et du jardin – sont traités de façon à participer à l'accord ou à l'harmonie de la nature et du paysage: ils deviennent vivants et se transforment en becs, mains, trompes ou insectes.
J'ai parlé plus haut du mur du lavoir en tant que curieuse créature engendrée par les champs alentour, la gargouille de la fontaine du jardin en est également une, mais en fer. Elle se voûte comme de la vermine rampante; heures heureuses de l'architecte, du ferronnier, des sœurs Bofarull. Fantastique.

ESGLESIA DE VISTABELLA

Neubau einer Kirche / Construction of a church / Construction d'une église
Vistabella, Tarragona, 1918–1924

Ein älterer Bewohner aus Vistabella erzählte mir seine Kindheitserinnerungen an Jujol, der bei ihm zu Hause wohnte, wenn er ins Dorf kam, um die Bauarbeiter an der Kirche zu beaufsichtigen: Jujol saß stundenlang am Tisch und betrachtete Pflanzen und Kräuter, die er draußen auf den Feldern gesammelt hatte; ein anderer erinnerte sich an Jujol in der Küche, wie er eine Tomate in der Mitte durchschnitt und den Kindern, zuerst am Tisch und dann mit der Tomate in der Hand hinter ihnen herlaufend, die Wunder ihres Inneren zu erklären suchte.

Ich glaube, die Kirche von Vistabella entstand aus dieser Haltung heraus; aus der Einstellung, die unmittelbare Umgebung sei etwas Wunderbares: Wolken, Felder, Bauernkarren, Früchte, Steine, Vögel, Insekten. Man kann sich leicht vorstellen, wie Jujol in der näheren Umgebung des Dorfes spazierengeht, auf Wegen, die oft von Mäuerchen aus aufgeschichteten Steinen gesäumt sind, die die Bauern auf den Feldern aufgelesen haben, damit man diese besser beackern kann. Man kann sich auch vorstellen, wie er solche Steine aufhebt, sie aufmerksam betrachtet und dann behutsam auf eine der Mauern legt.

Man muß nur das Wort »aufmerksam« durch »andächtig« ersetzen, um das baulich Wesentliche der Kirche von Vistabella zu erkennen: Die Steine von den umliegenden Äckern werden ausgewählt und aufeinandergeschichtet – der eine horizontal, der nächste vertikal –, damit der Betrachter sie vor dem Hintergrund des Himmels in der ganzen Fülle ihrer unverkennbaren Einzigartigkeit bewundern kann.

Die Kirche, das Bauwerk, die Architektur repräsentieren nichts anderes als den Altar, die offene Hand, auf dem Zeugnis für das Werk Gottes abgelegt wird. Diese Vorgehensweise ist bemerkenswert, da gewöhnlich genau das Gegenteil geschieht: Die Steine verschwinden im Innern der Mauern, die zum Teil ihrerseits wieder Bestandteil einer größeren gestalterischen Ordnung sind, in der die Kirche, die Architektur und die Architekten Bedeutendes zum Ausdruck bringen.

One of Vistabella's older residents told me of his childhood memories of Jujol, who used to stay in his house when he came to the village to oversee work on the church: Jujol would sit at the table for hours on end looking at the plants and herbs he had collected out in the fields. Another remembered Jujol in the kitchen, slicing a tomato in half and then trying to explain to the children, first seated at the table and then chasing after them, tomato in hand, the wonders of its insides.

I believe the Vistabella church arose out of this conviction, out of the view that the immediate environment – clouds, fields, farm carts, fruits, stones, birds, insects – was something wondrous. It is easy to picture Jujol exploring the local countryside, wandering down paths bordered with walls of piled-up stones gleaned from the fields to make them easier to plough. One may imagine him, too, picking up such stones, examining them closely and then placing them carefully on top of one of the walls.

By simply replacing the word »carefully« with »devoutly«, we have described the constructive essence of the church in Vistabella. Here, too, stones from the surrounding fields are selected and placed on top of each other – one horizontally, the next vertically –, so that the viewer can admire them, in the fullness of their unmistakable singularity, against the backdrop of the heavens.

Church, building, architecture are nothing other than an altar – an open palm – on which is deposited a testimony to God's work. The process is remarkable in the fact that the reverse is usually the case: stones are generally made to disappear inside walls, which are themselves often merely one aspect of a larger creative order through which the church, its architecture and its architects express a greater meaning.

Un vieil habitant de Vistabella m'a raconté ses souvenirs d'enfant relatifs à Jujol, qui habitait chez lui quand il venait au village pour surveiller la construction de l'église: Jujol était assis des heures durant à une table, examinant les plantes et les herbes qu'il avait ramassées dans les champs; un autre habitant se souvenait d'un jour où Jujol, qui se trouvait dans la cuisine, coupa une tomate en deux et voulut expliquer aux enfants les merveilles de l'intérieur de cette dernière, d'abord à table, puis courant derrière eux la tomate à la main.

Je crois que l'église de Vistabella a été créée à partir de cette attitude; à partir de l'idée que l'environnement immédiat est quelque chose de merveilleux: nuages, champs, charrettes, fruits, pierres, oiseaux, insectes. On imagine facilement Jujol se promenant dans les environs immédiats du village, sur des chemins souvent bordés de murets faits de pierres entassées les unes sur les autres, après avoir été ramassées dans les champs afin que ceux-ci soient plus facilement labourables. On peut également l'imaginer ramassant ces pierres, les examinant attentivement et les posant avec précaution sur l'un des murs.

Il suffit de remplacer le mot »attentivement« par »avec recueillement« pour discerner l'essentiel de l'architecture dans l'église de Vistabella: les pierres des champs environnants sont choisies et empilées les unes sur les autres – l'une horizontalement, l'autre verticalement –, afin que le spectateur puisse les admirer sur le fond du ciel dans toute la plénitude de son évidente unicité.

L'église, la construction, l'architecture n'est rien d'autre que l'autel – la main ouverte – sur lequel on témoigne de l'œuvre de Dieu. Cette façon de procéder est remarquable car c'est généralement le contraire qui se produit: les pierres disparaissent à l'intérieur des murs qui, de leur côté, sont de nouveau partiellement éléments d'un ordre créateur dans lequel l'église, l'architecture et les architectes expriment des choses importantes.

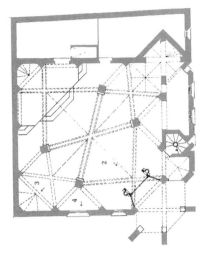

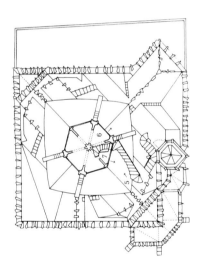

Die Kirche von Vistabella ist einer der seltenen Neubauten im Schaffen von Josep Maria Jujol. Sie wurde, wie andere seiner Bauwerke auch, ohne qualifizierte Arbeitskräfte errichtet, und wie so oft verfügte man auch hier nur über wenige und einfachste Materialien. Heute wird die Kirche von den Einwohnern Vistabellas liebevoll instand gehalten und ungewöhnlich zuvorkommend jedem geöffnet, der sie sich anschauen will. Während des Bürgerkriegs brannte die Kirche, und viele der Innenmalereien, die Jujol zusammen mit dem Maler Ramón Farré ausgeführt hatte, wurden durch den Rauch unkenntlich. Das Kernstück der malerischen Darstellung mit dem Altar des Heiligen Herzens in der Mitte wurde schwer beschädigt.

Vistabella church is one of the very small number of new buildings by Josep Maria Jujol. Like others of his works, it was built without skilled labour and employing, as was so often the case, just a few simple materials. Today the church is lovingly maintained by the residents of Vistabella, and opened with uncommon courtesy to all who wish to visit it. The church caught fire during the Civil War and much of the interior decoration, which Jujol painted together with the artist Ramón Farré, was spoilt beyond recognition by the smoke. The main section of the pictorial programme, in the centre of which stood the Altar of the Sacred Heart, suffered serious damage.

L'église de Vistabella est l'une des rares constructions neuves dans l'œuvre de Josep Maria Jujol. Elle a été, tout comme d'autres édifices, érigée sans main-d'œuvre spécialisée et, comme si souvent, on disposait là aussi de quelques rares et très simples matériaux. Aujourd'hui, l'église est affectueusement entretenue par les habitants de Vistabella et fort obligeamment ouverte à quiconque veut la visiter. Pendant la guerre civile, l'église a brûlé, et beaucoup des peintures intérieures exécutées par Jujol et le peintre Ramón Farré sont devenues méconnaissables à cause de la fumée. Le cœur de la représentation picturale, au milieu de laquelle se trouvait l'autel du Sacré-Cœur, a été gravement endommagé.

Turmtreppe und Glockenstuhl / Tower stairs and
belfry / Escalier de la tour et beffroi

Mauerkronen aus Feldsteinen / Wall crests made
of fieldstones / Couronnes murales en pierre de
taille

Wandmalerei und Gewölbe einer der Seiten-
kapellen / Wall paintings and vault in one of the
side chapels / Peinture murale et voûte de l'une
des chapelles latérales

Die Malerei wurde mit natürlichen Farben aufgetragen und zog sich wie eine Tätowierung durch den gesamten Innenraum der Kirche. Angefangen in einer Ecke oder einem anderen Ausgangspunkt, über Säulen, Nischen, Bögen, Wände und Türen fortschreitend, wurden unermüdlich neue Themen eingeführt, von denen man viele wiederfinden konnte, wenn man sich draußen umsah: Weinstöcke, Reben, Vögel, Wolken.

The painting was executed entirely in natural colours and covered the interior of the church like a tatoo, whereby an unceasing succession of new themes, many of which, such as vines, tendrils, birds, clouds, etc., could be found outside in the surrounding countryside – unfolded across pillars, recesses, arches, walls and doors.

La peinture a été réalisée avec des couleurs naturelles et s'étendait comme un tatouage dans tout l'intérieur de l'église. Commençant dans un coin ou un autre point de départ, elle continuait sur des colonnes, des niches, des arcs, des murs et des portes, tandis que de nouveaux thèmes étaient inlassablement introduits, on pourrait en retrouver beaucoup en regardant dehors: pieds de vigne, sarments, oiseaux, nuages.

CASA ANDREU

Umbauten / Alterations / Transformations
Els Pallaresos, Tarragona, 1920–1927

Jujol nahm an diesem Haus einige Umbauten vor, sie betrafen den Weinkeller, die Weinpressen, das Speisezimmer, die Treppe und weitere Objekte. Man beachte das Kupferblech, mit dem das Eingangstor beschlagen wurde. Wie andere Arbeiten Jujols zeigt es Dellen, Perforierungen, Falten und Inschriften, die dem Material Leben verleihen.
In der Casa Andreu finden sich außerdem zwei Deckenlampen, die aus dem zerstörten Umbau der Schwesternschule der Barmherzigen Karmeliterinnen in Tarragona gerettet wurden. Das Blumenwerk ist aus Konservendosenblech gefertigt.

Jujol here made a number of alterations to the wine cellar, presses, dining room, stairs and other objects. Noteworthy is the sheet copper studding the main door. As in other of Jujol's works, it bears the dents, perforations, folds and inscriptions which he uses to bring the material alive. Two ceiling lights inside the Casa Andreu were rescued from the destroyed alterations to the convent school of the Carmelite Sisters of Mercy in Tarragona. The flowers are made from tin cans.

Jujol a apporté à cette maison quelques modifications dans la cave, le pressoir, la salle à manger, l'escalier et autres objets. Remarquons la feuille de cuivre dont la porte d'entrée a été garnie. Comme dans d'autres travaux de Jujol, elle présente des creux, des perforations, des inscriptions et des plis grâce auxquels le matériel devient vivant.
Dans la Casa Andreu se trouvent en outre deux lampes de plafond rescapées des modifications détruites de l'école des carmélites de la Charité de Tarragone. Les fleurs ont été réalisées avec du métal pour boîtes de conserve.

TORRE SERRA-XAUS

Einfamilienhaus / Detached house / Maison individuelle
Sant Joan Despí, Barcelona, 1921–1927

Jujol baute dieses Wohnhaus im Auftrag
von Pere Xaus, einem Konstrukteur, mit
dem er gewöhnlich in Sant Joan Despí
zusammenarbeitete. Das in seiner Anlage und Ausführung eher unscheinbare
Haus weist dennoch eine merkwürdige,
ins Auge springende Anomalie auf. Eine
ganze Ecke des Gebäudes ist aus der geometrischen Form herausgelöst und steht
auf zwei Säulen wie ein gewaltiger aus-
gestellter Fuß hervor.
Der Torre Serra-Xaus war ursprünglich
als Einfamilienhaus geplant, wurde später jedoch in mehrere separate Wohnungen aufgeteilt.

Jujol was commissioned to build the
Torre Serra-Xaus by Pere Xaus, a design
engineer with whom he commonly
worked in Sant Joan Despí. The house,
its layout and design otherwise rather
unassuming, nevertheless reveals a strik-
ing anomaly: one entire corner is detached from the geometric whole and steps
forward like a huge foot on two stilts.
Torre Serra-Xaus was originally conceived as a detached residence, but was
later converted into several apartments.

Jujol a construit cette maison pour Pere
Xaus, un constructeur avec lequel il travaillait habituellement à Sant Joan Despí.
La maison, plutôt insignifiante de par sa
situation et sa réalisation, présente cependant une curieuse anomalie qui saute
aux yeux. Un coin entier du bâtiment est
détaché de la forme géométrique et s'a-
vance sur deux piliers comme un énorme
pied exposé.
La Torre Serra-Xaus, à l'origine projetée
comme maison individuelle, fut toutefois
divisée ultérieurement en plusieurs appartements.

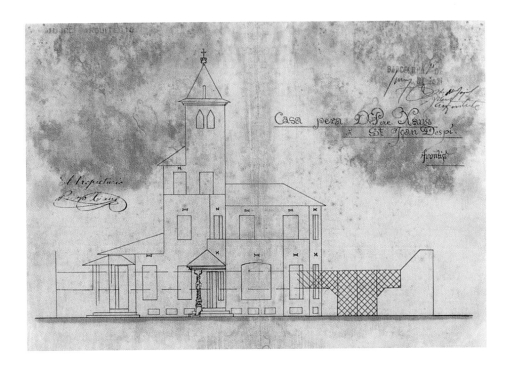

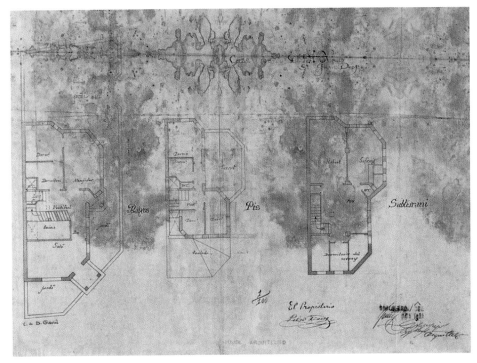

CASA PLANELLS

Neubau eines Wohnhauses / Construction of a residential building /
Construction d'un bâtiment d'habitation
Avinguda Diagonal 332, Barcelona, 1923

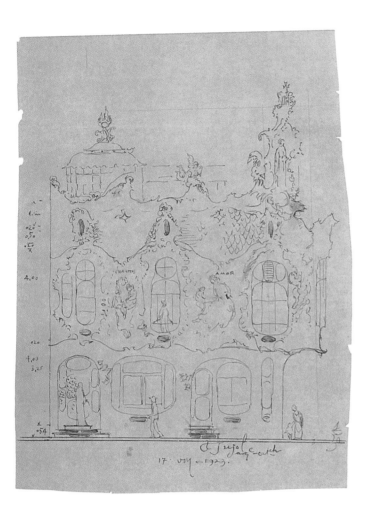

In einem der Vorentwürfe, die Jujol für den Bauherrn Evelí Planells gemacht hat, stellt er sich das Haus als einen Unterbau für ein großes Marienbild vor. Wie bei der Casa Negre ist Jujol – Architekt für Bauwerke unter der Protektion des Himmels – der Meinung, das Gebäude erlange Sinn und Würde, wenn es nichts weiter sei als der Unterbau für ein Madonnenbildnis an der Straßenecke Diagonal/Sicilia. Die Idee konnte nicht zu Ende geführt werden, und der Unterbau blieb unvollendet. Das oberste Stockwerk und die Dachterrasse wurden später gebaut, nicht von Jujol.

Die Casa Planells ist ein wunderschönes Haus, an dem sich kuriose Gleichzeitigkeiten mit der expressionistischen Architektur finden. Es ist auf sehr vielfältige Weise genutzt worden, als Wohnhaus, Pension, Laden- oder Bürogebäude, doch scheint es nie seine eigentlichen Bewohner gefunden zu haben. Es erweckt auf dieser von starkem Verkehr umtosten Straßenecke, zwischen seelenlosen Gebäuden zur Linken und Rechten, dennoch den Eindruck einer zarten, strahlenden alten Dame.

Es stimmt zwar nicht, aber ich habe mir immer vorgestellt, daß Jujol in diesem Haus gewohnt hat, daß er es während des Bürgerkriegs tagelang nicht verlassen hat und später, schon von den Jahren gebeugt, heraus auf die Straße trat, um sich zur Hochschule für Architektur zu begeben oder zu seinen kleinen Arbeiten außerhalb der Zeit. So haben viele von uns ihn in Erinnerung und auch einer seiner letzten Schüler, José A. Coderch: »Ich mag Gaudí, aber Jujol ist mir persönlich näher, vielleicht weil ich ihn gekannt habe und weil ich glaube, daß er sehr viel bedeutendere Bauwerke als Gaudí geschaffen hat.«

In one of the preparatory designs which Jujol made for his client Evelí Planells, he presented the house as the vehicle of a large image of the Virgin Mary. As in the Casa Negre, Jujol – architect of buildings under heavenly protection – believed that the building would assume meaning and value by serving as nothing less than the foundation for a portrait of the Madonna at the junction of Diagonal and Sicilia streets. The idea was not to be fully realized, and this foundation remained unfinished. The top floor and roof terrace were built later, but not by Jujol.

The Casa Planells is a beautiful house which bears curiously coincident similarities to Expressionist architecture. It has seen a variety of uses as a private residence, guest-house, furnished lodgings, shop and office building, but it never seems to have found its true owner. Despite the sea of heavy traffic raging before it and the soulless buildings to its left and right, it radiates the impression of a fragile but serene old lady. Although it was not so, I have always imagined Jujol living in the Casa Planells, staying in all day during the Civil War and later, bowed with age, setting off down the street to go the College of Architecture or to his small projects outside the boundaries of time. This is how many of us remember him, including one of his last students, José A. Coderch: »I like Gaudí, but Jujol is dearer to my heart, perhaps because I knew him personally, and because I believe he created works of much greater significance than those of Gaudí.«

Dans l'un des avant-projets conçus pour son client Evelí Planells, Jujol se représente la maison en tant que support pour une grande madone. Comme pour la Casa Negre, Jujol, architecte de constructions sous la protection du ciel, pense que le bâtiment acquiert un sens et une dignité s'il n'est rien d'autre qu'un support pour une madone au coin des rues Diagonal/Sicilia. L'idée n'a pas pu être menée à bien, et la construction est restée inachevée. L'étage supérieur et le toit-terrasse ont été construits ultérieurement, et pas par Jujol.

La Casa Planells est une magnifique maison où se trouvent de curieuses concomitances avec l'architecture expressionniste. Elle a été utilisée de multiples façons, comme maison d'habitation, pension, meublé, bâtiment commercial ou administratif, mais on dirait qu'elle n'a jamais trouvé ses véritables habitants. En ce coin de rue où la circulation déferle, entre des bâtiments sans âme à gauche et à droite, elle fait toutefois l'effet d'une vieille dame rayonnante.

Bien que cela ne soit pas exact, je me suis toujours imaginé que Jujol a habité dans la Casa Planells, qu'il ne l'a pas quittée des jours entiers pendant la guerre civile et que plus tard, déjà courbé par les ans, il est sorti dans la rue pour se rendre à l'École supérieure d'architecture ou à ses petits travaux hors du temps. Parmi nous, beaucoup se souviennent de lui de cette manière, de même que l'un de ses derniers élèves, José A. Coderch: »J'aime Gaudí, mais Jujol m'est personnellement plus proche, peut-étre parce que je l'ai connu et parce que je crois qu'il a créé des constructions beaucoup plus importantes que ne l'a fait Gaudí.«

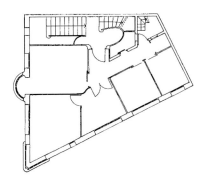 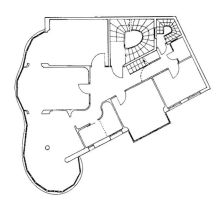 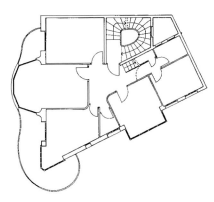

An dieser exponierten Ecke scheint die Casa Planells allen möglichen Winden ausgesetzt, die von Ost nach West die Diagonal hinunterfegen; und die Fassade, die des beschützenden Bildes entbehrt, gibt sich als knatternde Fahne unter dem Ansturm der Naturkräfte. Im Theater des Arbeiterpatronats sind ähnliche Bilder verwendet worden, nur daß es dort ein Sturm auf dem Ozean war.

The Casa Planells stands exposed on its street corner, buffeted by every east wind gusting down the Avenida Diagonal. Its façade, obliged to manage without its guardian icon, billows like a flag flapping under the onslaught of natural forces. Similar images were used in the Workers' Patronage theatre, where they took the form of a storm on the ocean.

A cet endroit exposé, on dirait que la Casa Planells est en butte à tous les vents possibles et imaginables qui balaient la rue Diagonal d'est en ouest; et la façade privée de l'image protectrice a l'air d'un drapeau claquant sous l'assaut des forces naturelles. Dans le Teatro del Patronato Obrero, des images semblables ont été employées, sauf qu'il y avait là une tempête sur l'océan.

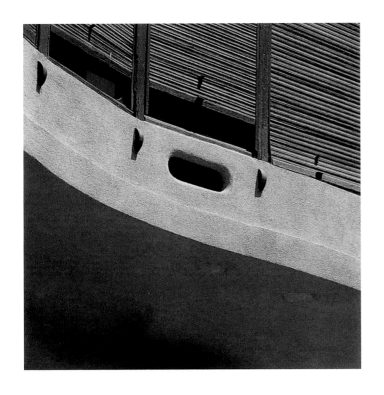

Treppenhaus und Säule im Erkerzimmer / Staircase and column in the projecting room / Escalier
et colonne dans la pièce en saillie

ERMITA DEL ROSER

Umbauten an der Eremitage / Alterations to the hermitage /
Transformation de l'ermitage
Vallmoll, Tarragona, 1925–1927

Auch in Vallmoll verfügte Jujol über wenig Material für die ihm übertragenen
Umbauarbeiten. Die Fassade und die Innenräume der Eremitage bemalte er zusammen mit dem aus Vallmoll stammen-
den Maler Ramón Farré. In die Fußböden
aus rolliertem Portlandzement wurden
Marmorstücke eingelegt. Es handelt sich
hierbei um eine – bisher wenig beachtete
– außergewöhnliche Arbeit. Mit Blick auf
die in den Marmor oder Zement eingra-
vierten Zeichnungen ist es erstaunlich,
was aus diesen bescheidenen Materialien gemacht worden ist, aus den Farben
und aus der Geometrie, die das Material
in Beziehung zu den Räumen setzt.

In Vallmoll, too, Jujol had few materials
at his disposal for the alterations assigned
to him. The façade and interiors of the
hermitage he painted together with the
artist Ramón Farré, who came from Vallmoll. The floors of rolled Portland
cement were tiled with pieces of marble,
whereby the drawings scored into the
marble and cement represent an
extraordinary – and previously rather
neglected – achievement, in view of
what has been made out of such modest
materials, out of their colour and out of
the geometry which relates the material
to the space around it.

A Vallmoll aussi, Jujol disposait de peu
de matériaux pour les transformations
qui lui étaient confiées. Il a peint la façade et l'intérieur de l'ermitage en collaboration avec le peintre Ramón Farré qui
était originaire de Vallmoll. Des morceaux de marbre ont été incrustés dans
les sols en ciment Portland roulé. Il s'agit
là d'un travail extraordinaire – jusqu'ici
peu remarqué – en ce qui concerne les
dessins gravés sur le marbre ou sur le ciment, si l'on considère ce qui a été fait
avec ces modestes matériaux, les couleurs et la géométrie établissant un rap-
port entre les matériaux et les pièces.

SANTUARI DE MONTFERRI

Heiligtum der Jungfrau von Montserrat / Shrine of the Blessed Virgin of Montserrat /
Sanctuaire de la Vierge de Montserrat
Montferri, Tarragona, 1926–1935

Montferri ist ein Dorf von zweihundert Einwohnern und liegt in dem Dreieck Valls-Vendrell-Tarragona. Die Landschaft besticht durch ihre zeitlose Ausgewogenheit und beherbergt die meisten ländlichen Arbeiten Jujols: Els Pallaresos, Vistabella, Vallmoll, Bonastre.

Montferri kommt im Gesamtwerk Jujols eine besondere Bedeutung zu. Die Arbeit beginnt 1929 und wird 1935 unterbrochen. Sie beginnt, als Jujol fünfzig Jahre alt ist, und wird unterbrochen, als er sechsundfünfzig Jahre alt ist; das heißt, die Arbeit fällt in einen Lebensabschnitt, in dem ein Architekt sich für gewöhnlich Kenntnisse und Erfahrungen zugute halten kann und den Voraussetzungen genügt, um ein ganz persönliches Werk in Angriff zu nehmen.

Das Heiligtum steht an hervorragender Stelle auf der Nase einer felsigen Anhöhe, und zu seinen Füßen breiten sich rundum kultivierte Flächen mit Weinstöcken und Mandelbäumen aus. Der Bau ist der Heiligen Jungfrau von Montserrat gewidmet, und die Möglichkeit, einen der Marienverehrung zugedachten Neubau zu gestalten und auszuführen, war für Josep Maria Jujol zweifellos eine außergewöhnliche Gelegenheit, berufliche Kenntnis und Sensibilität in den Dienst seiner tiefen religiösen Überzeugung zu stellen.

Die Mittel, mit denen das Bauwerk – soweit Jujol es fertigstellen konnte – errichtet wurde, die von der gleichen Beschränkung und Kargheit zeugen, wie wir sie von den meisten anderen seiner Werke kennen, sind ebenso wie die Landschaft um Tarragona wesentlicher Bestandteil der Jujolschen Architektur.

Alle Faktoren, die in Montferri zusammenkommen, persönliche Umstände, Lage, Bestimmung des Bauwerks, Materialien und selbst der schmerzvolle Abbruch der Bauarbeiten, machen das Heiligtum der Jungfrau von Montserrat zu einem entscheidenden, paradigmatischen Werk in der beruflichen Laufbahn des Architekten Jujol.

Montferri is a village of two hundred inhabitants which lies within the triangle between Valls, Vendrell and Tarragona. The landscape exudes a timeless harmony and is home to the majority of Jujol's rural works: Els Pallaresos, Vistabella, Vallmoll, Bonastre.

Montferri commands a particular status amongst Jujol's works. Work began in 1929 and was interrupted in 1935. It began when Jujol was fifty and was interrupted when he was fifty-six; in other words, it fell into that period of an architect's life when he can usually pride himself on his practical experience and bring the maturity necessary to a highly personal creation.

The shrine occupies a prominent position on the snout of a rocky elevation, with cultivated areas of vineyards and almond orchards spread at its feet. The building is dedicated to the Blessed Virgin of Montserrat, and the chance to design and execute a new building intended for the veneration of the Virgin Mary undoubtedly offered Josep Maria Jujol an extraordinary opportunity to place his professional expertise and sensitivity at the service of his profound religious beliefs.

The resources with which the shrine – or what Jujol was able to complete of it – was built, and which were as limited and meagre as in the case of most of Jujol's works, represent – like the Tarragona landscape itself – an essential component of Jujolian architecture.

All the factors which came together in Montferri – personal circumstances, location, building brief, materials, even the painful abandonment of construction work – make the shrine to the Blessed Virgin of Montserrat a decisive, paradigmatic work in the professional career of the architect Josep Maria Jujol.

Montferri est un village de deux cents habitants situé dans le triangle Valls-Vendrell-Tarragone. Le paysage séduit par un équilibre intemporel et abrite la plupart des travaux ruraux de Jujol: Els Pallaresos, Vistabella, Vallmoll, Bonastre. Montferri revêt une importance particulière dans l'ensemble de l'œuvre de Jujol. Les travaux commencent en 1929 et sont interrompus en 1935. Ils commencent alors que Jujol a cinquante ans et sont interrompus alors qu'il en a cinquante-six; cela signifie que la construction a lieu dans une période de vie au cours de laquelle un architecte peut habituellement profiter de connaissances et d'expériences et remplit les conditions pour entreprendre une œuvre très personnelle.

Le sanctuaire se trouve à un endroit remarquable au sommet d'une hauteur rocheuse, et des surfaces cultivées, des pieds de vigne et des amandiers s'étalent à ses pieds. La construction est dédiée à la Vierge de Montserrat, et la possibilité de concevoir et de réaliser une nouvelle construction destinée au culte marial était sans aucun doute pour Josep Maria Jujol une occasion extraordinaire de mettre ses connaissances professionnelles et sa sensibilité au service de sa profonde conviction religieuse.

Les moyens avec lesquels la construction a été réalisée – dans la mesure où Jujol a pu la terminer –, et qui témoignent des mêmes restrictions et de la même pauvreté que la plupart de ses autres œuvres, sont partie intégrante de l'architecture jujolienne au même titre que le paysage des environs de Tarragone.

Tout ce qui est réuni à Montferri, les circonstances personnelles, le site, la destination du bâtiment, les matériaux et même la douloureuse interruption des travaux font du sanctuaire de la Vierge de Montserrat une œuvre décisive, paradigmatique dans la carrière de l'architecte Josep Maria Jujol.

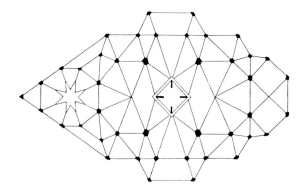

Der Bürgerkrieg in Spanien vereitelte das Heranwachsen zu vollblütiger Reife; und man weiß um die Niedergeschlagenheit Jujols, der bei mehreren Besuchen nach dem Bürgerkrieg erkennen mußte, daß das Marienheiligtum zusehends verfiel. Trotz allem ist dieses Bauwerk auf felsiger Höhe inmitten der lichtdurchfluteten Landschaft, halbfertig nur, ein überwältigendes architektonisches Zeugnis.

The Civil War in Spain thwarted its growth to full-blooded maturity, and we know of Jujol's dejection as he was forced to recognize, in the course of several visits following the Civil War, that his shrine was rapidly decaying. Despite everything, the building, half-finished on a rocky hillside amidst a floodlit landscape, remains an overwhelming architectural achievement.

La guerre civile espagnole fit échouer la montée vers la pleine maturité; et l'on sait que Jujol fut déprimé quand il lui fallut reconnaître, lors de plusieurs visites après la guerre civile, que le sanctuaire dédié à Marie tombait visiblement en ruines. Perchée sur une éminence rocheuse au milieu d'un paysage baigné de lumière, et seulement à demi achevée, cette construction est malgré tout un ouvrage architectonique grandiose.

Bogen und Gewölbe im »Cambril de la Verge« /
Arches and vaults in the »Cambril de la Verge« /
Arc et voûte dans le »Cambril de la Verge«

Da Baumaterial überaus knapp war, entschloß sich Jujol, die ganze Konstruktion auf der Grundlage von Blockbausteinen zu errichten, die er an Ort und Stelle aus Zement, Sand und Schlacke, die von der nahen Bahnstation Salomó stammte, herstellen ließ.

Die Materialknappheit ließ Jujol auch alte Stahlmatratzen als Armierung der zementierten Mauern verwenden, welche die gesamte Anlage umschließen sollten, aber auch nur zum Teil fertiggestellt wurden. Die Biegsamkeit des Stahlnetzes findet ihren Ausdruck in der Form der nach innen und außen, nach oben und unten ausgebeulten Mauern.

Since building materials were in exceedingly short supply, Jujol decided to base the entire construction on blocks made on site from cement, sand, and cinder obtained from the nearby Salomó railway station.

The same shortage of materials led Jujol to use old sprung mattresses to reinforce the cement walls which were to encircle the entire complex, but which were only partially completed. The elasticity of their springs is stated in the inward and outward, upward and downward bulging of the walls.

Comme les matériaux de construction étaient rares, Jujol décida d'ériger toute la construction sur la base de blocs qu'il faisait faire sur place avec du ciment, du sable et de la scorie provenant de la gare voisine de Salomó.

La rareté des matériaux poussa Jujol à employer de vieux sommiers comme armatures pour les murs cimentés qui devaient entourer tout le site, mais qui ne furent terminés, eux aussi, que partiellement. La souplesse du treillis d'acier s'exprime dans la forme des murs bosselés vers l'intérieur et vers l'extérieur, vers le haut et vers le bas.

Derzeit wird an der Kirche weitergebaut. Hohe
Lehrgerüste überragen die Baufragmente aus den
dreißiger Jahren.
Construction work on the church has been re-
sumed. High centrings rise above the structural
fragments dating from the 1930s.
Aujourd'hui, les travaux se poursuivent dans l'é-
glise. De grands cintres de charpente dominent
les fragments des années trente.

CASA JUJOL

Wohnhaus des Architekten / The architect's house / La maison de l'architecte
Sant Joan Despí, Barcelona, 1932

Das Haus, das Jujol für sich selbst in Sant Joan Despí gebaut hat, ist ein niedriges Gebäude, das zwei Wohnungen in Form eines »L« an ihren kurzen Seiten zusammenlegt und so einen symmetrischen Grundriß ergibt. Das schlichte Bauwerk ist weiß verputzt, Fenster und Türen sind mit blauen Sgraffiti umrahmt, wobei die Symmetrie immer wieder unterbrochen wurde, ebenso wie die Mauerkronen am oberen Teil des Hauses, die fragmentarisch wirken.

The low-storeyed house which Jujol built for himself in Sant Joan Despí is based upon two L-shaped apartments, which are joined along their shorter sides to give a symmetrical ground plan. This simple building is plastered white; windows and doors are framed with blue sgraffiti, whereby their symmetry is constantly interrupted. The same fragmented impression is recreated in the coping on the upper half of the house.

La maison que Jujol a construit pour sa famille à Sant Joan Despí est un bâtiment bas qui réunit deux appartements en forme de »L« sur ses petits côtés et a ainsi un plan symétrique. La construction simple a un crépi blanc; les portes et les fenêtres sont entourées de sgraffites bleus; la symétrie a été interrompue à plusieurs reprises, de même que le couronnement des murs dans la partie supérieure de la maison, qui semblent fragmentaires.

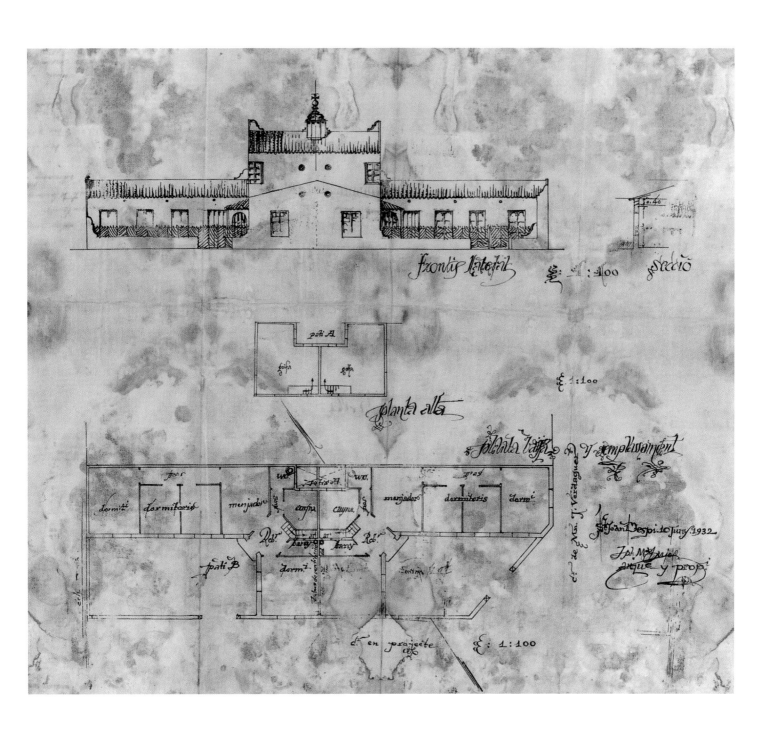

frontis lateral   1 : 100   sacció

pati A

fossa   fossa

1:100

planta alta

planta baixa y emplaçament

dormiti   dormitoris   menjador   wc   wc   menjador   dormitoris   dormi

cuina   cuina

Rcb.   barri   barri   Rcb.

pati B   dormt   cuina

en projecte   1 : 100

S. Joan Despí 10 juny 1932

Jph Mª Jujol
arqtue y propi

Tabernakel und Taufbecken der Kirche / Tabernacle and font of the church /
Tabernacle et fonts baptismaux de l'église
Bonastre, Tarragona, 1941–1944

Der Tabernakel scheint aus einem Behältnis mit einer ursprünglich ganz anderen Funktion gefertigt zu sein, zumindest jedoch mit erkennbarer Gleichgültigkeit der äußeren Form gegenüber. Entscheidend ist, was daraus gemacht worden ist, um die äußere Form vergessen zu lassen und es in einen Tabernakel zu verwandeln: Engel, die Tür zum Allerheiligsten öffnet sich, schwingende Flügel, die Inschrift verschwindet, Malerei tut sich auf.

The tabernacle appears to have been created from a container destined for an entirely different purpose, or at least with a clear lack of regard for external form. What is significant, however, is the means by which Jujol has erased this outer form and transformed it into a tabernacle: angels, the door which opens onto the Sacraments, beating wings, the inscription disappears – painting unfolds.

On dirait que le tabernacle a été fabriqué à partir d'un récipient pour un tout autre usage, pour le moins, toutefois, avec une indifférence visible vis-à-vis de la forme extérieure. L'essentiel est ce qui a été réalisé avec pour faire oublier la forme extérieure et le transformer en tabernacle: Anges, la porte du saint des saints s'ouvre, ailes vibrantes, l'inscription disparaît, la peinture se déploie.

Das Taufbecken stellt Jujol auf einen ir-
gendwoher ergatterten Sockel und baut
um ihn herum ein Podium, dergestalt,
daß das Taufbecken in einem Einschnitt
steht und mit dem Podium zum Kapel-
lenraum hin abschließt. Zwei Teile der
Abdeckung entfalten sich wie majestäti-
sche Schwingen aus mit Goldbronze be-
maltem Holz. Im geöffneten Zustand
schirmen sie den Raum ab, in dem die
Taufzeremonie stattfindet, und enthüllen
in bläulichem Schimmer das Taufbecken
mit dem geweihten Wasser.

Jujol places the font on a pedestal which he has unearthed from somewhere, and builds a raised podium up around it, so that the font stands in a recess with the podium behind it. Two sections of the cover unfold like majestic wings of gilded wood. When opened they screen the area in which the baptism ceremony is taking place, and unveil the shimmering blue of the font with the consecrated water.

Jujol pose les fonts baptismaux sur un socle trouvé dans un endroit quelconque et construit autour une estrade de façon à ce que les fonts baptismaux se trouvent dans un renfoncement et se terminent avec l'estrade vers la chapelle. Deux parties de la couverture se déplient comme de majestueuses ailes en bois peint avec du bronze d'or. Quand elles sont ouvertes, elles protègent l'espace dans lequel se déroule la cérémonie et dévoilent dans une lueur bleuâtre les fonts baptismaux avec l'eau bénite.

CHRONOLOGIE / CHRONOLOGY

1879

Josep Maria Jujol Gibert wird am 16. September als Sohn von Andrés Jujol und Teresa Gibert in Tarragona geboren.

Josep Maria Jujol Gibert is born in Tarragona on 16 September, the son of Andrés Jujol and Teresa Gibert.

Josep Maria Jujol Gibert naît le 16 septembre à Tarragone. Il est le fils d'Andrés Jujol et de Teresa Gibert.

1897

Studien an der wissenschaftlichen Fakultät, Besuch der Provinzhochschule für Architektur

Studies at the Science faculty, attends the Provincial College of Architecture

Etudie à la Faculté des sciences, fréquente l'École supérieure provinciale d'architecture

1901

Arbeit im Studio von Antoni Maria Gallissà
Sgraffito und Geländer für die Treppe der Casa Gallissà

Works in Antoni Maria Gallissà's studio Sgraffiti and railings for the Casa Gallissà

Travaille dans le studio de Antoni Maria Gallissà
Sgraffites et rampe d'escalier pour la Casa Gallissà

1902

Zusammenarbeit mit Gallissà an den Sgraffiti eines Wohnhauses und den Dekorationen der Carrer de Ferran in Barcelona
Zusammenarbeit mit Josep Font i Gumà am Dreifaltigkeitsaltar von Santa Maria del Mar in Barcelona

Assists Gallissà on sgraffiti for a residential building and on decorations for the Carrer de Ferran in Barcelona
Assists Josep Font i Gumà on the Holy Trinity Altar for the Church of Santa Maria del Mar in Barcelona

Collaboration avec Gallissà aux sgraffites d'une maison d'habitation et aux décorations du Carrer de Ferran à Barcelone
Collaboration avec Josep Font i Gumà à l'autel de la Trinité de Santa Maria del Mar à Barcelone

1904

Zusammenarbeit mit Josep Font i Gumà beim Umbau des Athenäums von Barcelona (bis 1906)

Redevelopment of the Barcelona Athenaeum in collaboration with Josep Font i Gumà (until 1906)

Transforme l'athénée de Barcelone en collaboration avec Josep Font i Gumà (jusqu'en 1906)

1905

Mosaiken für die Basilika Padre Nuestro de Jerusalén

Mosaics for the Padre Nuestro de Jerusalén Basilica

Mosaïques pour la basilique Padre Nuestro de Jerusalén

1906

Abschlußarbeit im Fachbereich Architektur unter dem Titel »Entwurf von Thermalbädern«
Zusammenarbeit mit Antoni Gaudí an der Casa Batlló in Barcelona
Mehrfamilienhaus in der Carrer Tapioles in Barcelona (fertiggestellt 1907)

Architectural thesis: »Design for a thermal spa«
Assists Antoni Gaudí on the Casa Batlló in Barcelona
Apartment house in Carrer Tapioles in Barcelona (completed 1907)

Travail de fin d'études dans la section architecture: »Projet de thermes«
Collaboration avec Antoni Gaudí à la Casa Batlló
Immeuble collectif à Carrer Tapioles à Barcelone (achevé en 1907)

1908

Zusammenarbeit mit Gaudí an der Casa Milà und – bis 1926 – an der Sagrada Familia in Barcelona
Ornamentierung der Kirche von Alcover
Bemalungen der alten Stadtmauer von Barcelona
Theater des Arbeiterpatronats in Tarragona

Assists Gaudí on the Casa Milà and – until 1926 – the Sagrada Familia in Barcelona
Ornamentation of the church in Alcover
Murals on the old Barcelona city wall
Theatre of the Workers' Patronage in Tarragona

Collaboration avec Gaudí à la Casa Milà et – jusqu'en 1926 – à la Sagrada Familia à Barcelone
Décoration de l'église d'Alcover
Peintures du vieux mur d'enceinte de Barcelone
Théâtre du patronat ouvrier à Tarragone

1909

Ernennung zum stellvertretenden Dozenten an der Architekturschule
Torre San Salvador in Barcelona (fertiggestellt 1915)
Entwurf der Teixidor-Mühle in Girona

Appointed deputy lecturer at the College of Architecture
Torre San Salvador in Barcelona (completed 1915)
Project for the Teixidor flour mill in Girona

Nomination au poste de chargé de cours adjoint à l'École d'architecture
Torre San Salvador à Barcelone (achevé en 1915)
Projet du moulin Teixidor à Gerona

1910

Entwurf von Mosaiken für die Casa Escofet in Barcelona
Zusammenarbeit mit Antoni Gaudí bei der Restaurierung der Kathedrale von Palma de Mallorca
Straßenleuchten aus Anlaß der Gedenkfeiern für Jaume Balmes in Barcelona in Zusammenarbeit mit Gaudí

Design of mosaics for the Casa Escofet in Barcelona
Assists Antoni Gaudí on the restoration of the cathedral of Palma de Mallorca
Street lights for the centenary of Jaume Balmes in Barcelona in collaboration with Gaudí

Projet de mosaïques pour la Casa Escofet à Barcelone
Collaboration avec Antoni Gaudí lors de la restauration de la cathédrale de Palma de Majorque
Collaboration avec Gaudí aux réverbères pour le centenaire de Jaume Balmes à Barcelone

1911

Ladeneinrichtung der Casa Mañach in Barcelona
Entwürfe für die Casa de Família in Barcelona
Umbauten an der Fabrik Mañach in Barcelona
Arbeit am Park Güell in Barcelona in Zusammenarbeit mit Gaudí (bis 1913)

Interior of the Casa Mañach shop in Barcelona
Designs for the Casa de Família in Barcelona
Alterations to the Mañach factory in Barcelona
Work on the Park Güell in Barcelona in collaboration with Gaudí (until 1913)

Intérieur du magasin Casa Mañach à Barcelone
Projet pour la Casa Família à Barcelone
Transformation de l'usine Mañach à Barcelone
Collaboration avec Gaudí aux travaux du Parc Güell à Barcelone (jusqu'à 1913)

1912

Entwürfe für Arbeiten an der Kathedrale von Tarragona

Designs for the cathedral in Tarragona

Projets pour la cathédrale de Tarragone

1913

Ernennung zum ordentlichen Dozenten an der Hochschule für Architektur im Fach »Kopie und Detail«
Fahrstuhl der Casa Iglésias in Barcelona
Torre de la Creu in Sant Joan Despí (fertiggestellt 1916)
Innenarbeiten an der Pfarrkirche von Constantí
Stadtentwicklungsplan für Les Corts

Appointed full lecturer at the College of Architecture for the subject »Copy and Detail«
Lift in the Casa Iglésias in Barcelona
Torre de la Creu in Sant Joan Despí (completed 1916)
Interior for the parish church of Constantí
Development plan for Les Corts

Nommé chargé de cours titulaire à l'école supérieure d'architecture pour la discipline »Copie et détail«
Ascenseur de la Casa Iglésias à Barcelone
Torre de la Creu à Sant Joan Despí (achevée en 1916)
Travaux intérieurs dans l'église paroissiale de Constantí
Plan d'urbanisme pour Les Corts

1914

Mehrfamilienhaus Casa Ximenis in Tarragona
Wohnhaus in Poble Sec
Umbau der Casa Bofarull in Els Pallaresos (abgeschlossen 1931)

Casa Ximenis (apartment house) in Tarragona
Residential building in Poble Sec
Alterations to the Casa Bofarull in Els Pallaresos (finished in 1931)

Immeuble collectif Casa Ximenis à Tarragone
Maison à Poble Sec
Transformation de la Casa Bofarull à Els Pallaresos (achevée en 1931)

1915

Umbau der Casa Negre in Sant Joan Despí (fertiggestellt 1926)
Haus für Vicente Dei i Giu in Sant Joan Despí
Entwurf eines Wohnhauses in Gràcia

Alterations to the Casa Negre in Sant Joan Despí (completed 1926)
House for Vicente Dei i Giu in Sant Joan Despí
Project for a residential building in Gràcia

Transformation de la Casa Negre à Sant Joan Despí (achevée en 1926)
Maison pour Vicente Dei i Giu à Sant Joan Despí
Projet de maison à Gràcia

1916

Fabrikhalle Mañach in Barcelona (1918 fertiggestellt)

Mañach factory wing in Barcelona (completed 1918)

Bâtiment d'usine Mañach à Barcelone (achevé en 1918)

1917

Torre Queralt in Barcelona
Schule und Rathaus in Els Pallaresos (fertiggestellt 1920)
Glockenturm der Kirche von Creixell de Mar
Umbau eines Landhauses in La Budallera
Erweiterung der Casa Xatruc in La Canonja

Torre Queralt in Barcelona
School and town hall in Els Pallaresos (completed 1920)
Bell-tower for the church in Creixell de Mar
Alterations to a country house in La Budallera
Project for extensions to the Casa Xatruc in La Canonja

Torre Queralt à Barcelone
Ecole et mairie à Els Pallaresos (achevées en 1920)
Clocher de l'église de Creixell de Mar
Transformation d'une résidence à La Budallera
Projet d'agrandissement de la Casa Xatruc à La Canonja

1918

Neubau der Kirche von Vistabella (fertiggestellt 1924)
Arbeiten an der Casa Bruguera (abgeschlossen 1922)

Vistabella church (completed 1924)
Alterations to the Casa Bruguera in Barcelona (completed 1922)

Eglise de Vistabella (achevée en 1924)
Modifications de la Casa Bruguera (achevées en 1922)

1919

Kapelle für die Karmeliterkirche in Tarragona
Entwurf für die Casa Iglésias in Tarragona
Entwurf zum Umbau der Fabrik Casanovas in Barcelona

Chapel for the Carmelite church in Tarragona
Designs for the Casa Iglésias in Tarragona
Designs for remodelling the Casanovas factory in Barcelona

Chapelle de l'église des Carmes à Tarragone
Projet de la Casa Iglésias à Tarragone
Projet pour la transformation de l'usine Casanovas à Barcelone

1920

Umbauten an der Casa Andreu in Els Pallaresos (fertiggestellt 1927)
Arbeiten an der Casa Maluquer in Sant Joan Despí
Entwurf einer Leuchte für die Dominikanerkirche von Barcelona

Alterations to the Casa Andreu in Els Pallaresos (completed 1927)
Alterations to the Casa Maluquer in Sant Joan Despí
Lamp design for the Dominican church in Barcelona

Transformation de la Casa Andreu à Els Pallaresos (achevée en 1927)
Travaux dans la Casa Maluquer à Sant Joan Despí
Projet de lampe pour l'église des Dominicains à Barcelone

1921

Torre Serra-Xaus in Sant Joan Despí (fertiggestellt 1927)
Entwurf eines Stuhles für den Abt des Klosters von Montserrat
Renovierung des Gebäudes der Reverendes Oblates in Barcelona
Stall und Wohnhaus für Joan Camprubí Torrent in Sant Joan Despí

Torre Serra-Xaus in Sant Joan Despí (completed 1927)
Design of a chair for the Abbot of Montserrat Monastery
Alterations to the building of the Reverendes Oblates in Barcelona
Stable and house for Joan Camprubí Torrent in Sant Joan Despí

Torre Serra-Xaus à Sant Joan Despí (achevé en 1927)
Projet de chaise pour l'abbé du cloître de Montserrat
Transformation du bâtiment des oblates à Barcelone
Etable et maison pour Joan Camprubí Torrent à Sant Joan Despí

1922

Erster Entwurf für die Casa Planells
Wohnhaus an der Ecke Independencia/Carrer Enamorats in Barcelona
Häuser für Zacaries Donate Sorribes, Ricard Sigalés Porta und Vicenc Margarit Sabaté in Sant Joan Despí
Erweiterung des Hauses von Antoni Llach Roca in Sant Joan Despí

First design for the Casa Planells
Residential house on the corner of Independencia/Carrer Enamorats in Barcelona
Houses for Zacaries Donate Sorribes, Ricard Sigalés Porta and Vicenc Margarit Sabaté in Sant Joan Despí
Extensions to the home of Antoni Llach Roca in Sant Joan Despí

Premier projet pour la Casa Planells
Maison au coin des rues Independencia/Carrer Enamorats à Barcelone
Maisons individuelles pour Zacaries Donate Sorribes, Ricard Sigalés Porta et Vicenc Margarit Sabaté à Sant Joan Despí
Agrandissement de la maison d'Antoni Llach Roca à Sant Joan Despí

1923

Neubau der Casa Planells in Barcelona
Wettbewerbsentwurf für eine neue Stadt-
bücherei in Barcelona
Wohnhäuser für Jaume Babot und Joan
Manadé in Sant Joan Despí

Casa Planells in Barcelona
Competition entry for a new public library in Barcelona
Houses for Jaume Babot and Joan Manadé in Sant Joan Despí

Casa Planells à Barcelone
Projet-concours pour une bibliothèque
publique à Barcelone
Maisons individuelles pour Jaume Babot
et Joan Manadé à Sant Joan Despí

1924

Lehrauftrag an der Gewerbeschule
Umbau des Regionalzentrums in Sant
Joan Despí
Wohnhaus für Eduardo Buján in Sant
Joan Despí

Lectureship at the Technical College
Alterations to the Regional Centre in Sant
Joan Despí
House for Eduardo Buján in Sant Joan
Despí

Chargé de cours à l'Ecole technique
Centre régional à Sant Joan Despí
Maison individuelle pour Eduardo Buján
à Sant Joan Despí

1925

Umbauten an der El Roser Eremitage in
Vallmoll (beendet 1927)
Wohnhäuser für Josep Pey Vives und Ra-
mon Turmó in Sant Joan Despí
Renovierung der Fassade des Hauses von
Antoni Batllorí in Sant Joan Despí

Alterations to the El Roser hermitage in
Vallmoll (completed 1927)
Detached houses for Josep Pey Vives and
Ramon Turmó in Sant Joan Despí
Restoration of the façade of the home of
Antoni Batllorí in Sant Joan Despí

Transformation de l'ermitage de El Roser
à Vallmoll (achevée en 1927)
Maisons individuelles pour Josep Pey
Vives et Ramon Turmó à Sant Joan Despí
Rénovation de la façade de la maison
d'Antoni Battlorí à Sant Joan Despí

1926

Ernennung zum Stadtarchitekten von
Sant Joan Despí
Springbrunnen in Brafim
Stadtplanungsentwurf für das Samontà-
Viertel in Sant Joan Despí
Malereien an der Kirche des Heiligen
Franziskus in Tarragona
Entwurf zum Wiederaufbau des römi-
schen Amphitheaters in Tarragona
Marientempel in Montferri (Arbeiten
1935 eingestellt)
Renovierung der Eremitage Nostra
Senyora de Lloreto in Renau
Wohnhaus für Joan Badell Farrés in Sant
Joan Despí
Umbauten und Sgraffiti der Casa Rovira
in Sant Joan Despí

Appointed Municipal Architect of Sant
Joan Despí
Fountain in Brafim
Urban development project for the
Samontà district of Sant Joan Despí
Paintings in the church of Sant Francesc
in Tarragona
Designs for the reconstruction of the Ro-
man amphitheatre in Tarragona
Shrine to the Blessed Virgin of Montferri
(construction interrupted in 1935)
Renovations to the Nostra Senyora de
Lloreto Hermitage in Renau
House for Joan Badell Farrés in Sant Joan
Despí
Alterations and sgraffiti for the Casa Rov-
ira in Sant Joan Despí

Nommé architecte municipal de Sant
Joan Despí
Jet d'eau à Brafim
Projet d'urbanisme pour le quartier de
Samontà à Sant Joan Despí
Peintures dans l'église de Sant Francesc à
Tarragone
Projet de rénovation de l'amphithéâtre
romain à Tarragone
Sanctuaire marial de Montferri (construc-
tion interrompue en 1935)
Rénovation de l'ermitage de Nostra Se-
nyora de Lloreto à Renau
Maison individuelle pour Badell Farrès à
Sant Joan Despí
Transformations et sgraffites de la Casa
Rovira à Sant Joan Despí

1927

Heirat mit Teresa Gibert
Bezug des Ateliers in der Rambla de Catalunya 79 in Barcelona
Umbauten an der Casa Solé in Els Pallaresos
Zeughaus für die Weltausstellung in Barcelona in Zusammenarbeit mit Andrés Calzada
Arbeiten für die Kapelle des Heiligen Christophorus in Barcelona
Doppelhaus für Modest Tàpias in Sant Joan Despí
Häuser für Jaume Vives, Vicenc Roca Amigó und Josep Pey in Sant Joan Despí
Umbau des Gutshauses Casa Po Cardona in Sant Joan Despí
Ausbau des Hauses von Francesc Joaquim in Sant Joan Despí

Marries Teresa Gibert
Moves into studio at Rambla de Catalunya 79 in Barcelona
Alterations to the Casa Solé in Els Pallaresos
Arsenal for the International Exhibition in Barcelona in collaboration with Andrés Calzada
Work on the chapel of Sant Cristòfol del Regomir in Barcelona
Semi-detached residence for Modest Tàpias in Sant Joan Despí
Houses for Jaume Vives, Vicenc Roca Amigó and Josep Pey in Sant Joan Despí
Alterations to the Casa Po Cardona manor in Sant Joan Despí
Extensions to the home of Francesc Joaquim in Sant Joan Despí

Epouse Teresa Gibert
Emménage dans l'atelier de la Rambla de Catalunya 79 à Barcelone
Transformation de la Casa Solé à Els Pallaresos
Arsenal pour l'exposition universelle de Barcelone en collaboration avec Andrés Calzada
Projets pour la chapelle de Sant Cristòfol del Regomir à Barcelone
Maison à deux logements pour Modest Tàpias à Sant Joan Despí
Maisons pour Jaume Vives, Vicenc Roca Amigó et Josep Pey à Sant Joan Despí
Transformation du domaine Casa Po Cardona à Sant Joan Despí
Agrandissement de la maison Francesc Joaquim à Sant Joan Despí

1928

Zweimonatige Reise durch Italien
Gedenkbrunnen zur Weltausstellung auf der Plaça d' Espanya in Barcelona
Torre Camprubí in Cornellà de Llobregat

Two-month trip to Italy
Commemorative fountain for the International Exhibition at the Plaça d' Espanya in Barcelona
Torre Camprubí in Cornellà de Llobregat

Voyage de deux mois en Italie
Fontaine commémorative pour l'exposition universelle sur la Plaça d' Espanya à Barcelone
Torre Camprubí à Cornellà de Llobregat

1929

Umbau des Hauses von Joan Dot Carrera in Sant Joan Despí
Fassadenrenovierung der Casa Claramunt in Sant Joan Despí
Wohnhäuser für Teresa Vives und Ramon Turmó in Sant Joan Despí

Alterations to the home of Joan Dot Carrera in Sant Joan Despí
Façade of the Casa Claramunt in Sant Joan Despí
Houses for Teresa Vives and Ramon Turmó in Sant Joan Despí

Transformation de la maison de Joan Dot Carrera à Sant Joan Despí
Façade de la Casa Claramunt à Sant Joan Despí
Maisons individuelles pour Teresa Vives et Ramon Turmó à Sant Joan Despí

1930

Umbauten an der Fabrik Les Begudes in Sant Joan Despí
Entwurf einer Kapelle für Sant Magí in Brufaganya
Entwurf für den Umzug des Heiligen Kreuzes der Sankt-Lorenz-Kirche
Doppelhaus für José Carbonell in Sant Joan Despí
Erweiterung des Hauses von Baldiri Ollé in Sant Joan Despí
Wohnhaus für Llorenç Tarrés in Sant Joan Despí

Alterations to the Les Begudes factory in Sant Joan Despí
Chapel project for Sant Magí in Brufaganya
Designs for the parade of the Holy Cross for the church of Sant Llorenc
Semi-detached house for José Carbonell in Sant Joan Despí
Extensions to the home of Baldiri Ollé in Sant Joan Despí
House for Llorenç Tarrés in Sant Joan Despí

Transformation de l'usine Les Begudes à Sant Joan Despí
Projet de chapelle pour le sanctuaire de Sant Magí à Brufaganya
Projet pour la procession de la Croix de l'église Sant Llorenc
Maison à deux logements pour José Carbonell à Sant Joan Despí
Agrandissement de la Casa Baldiri Ollé à Sant Joan Despí
Maison individuelle pour Llorenç Tarrés à Sant Joan Despí

1931

Arbeiten in der Kirche von El Vendrell (beendet 1943)
Reparaturen im Vikariat von La Bispal del Penedès
Wohnhäuser für Josep Vila, Matías Zaragoza, Joan Oliach Martí und Isidre Calvet Gil in Sant Joan Despí

Work on the church of El Vendrell (completed 1943)
Repairs to the vicarage of La Bispal del Penedès
Houses for Josep Vila, Matías Zaragoza, Joan Oliach Martí and Isidre Calvet Gil in Sant Joan Despí

Travaux dans l'église de El Vendrell (terminés en 1943)
Travaux dans le vicariat de La Bispal del Penedès
Maisons individuelles pour Josep Vila, Matías Zaragoza, Joan Oliach Martí et Isidre Calvet Gil à Sant Joan Despí

1932

Doppelhaus Torre Jujol in Sant Joan Despí
Arbeiten an der Kirche von Sant Joan Despí (bis 1943)
Wohnhäuser für Mario Passani, Joan Manadé i Amigó, Antoni Brichfeus, Carles Gastó und Ramon Forcada in Sant Joan Despí

Torre Jujol (semi-detached house) in Sant Joan Despí
Work on the church of Sant Joan Despí (until 1943)
Houses for Mario Passani, Joan Manadé i Amigó, Antoni Brichfeus, Carles Gastó and Ramon Forcada in Sant Joan Despí

Maison à deux logements Torre Jujol à Sant Joan Despí
Travaux dans l'église de Sant Joan Despí (jusqu'en 1943)
Maisons individuelles pour Mario Passani, Joan Manadé i Amigó, Antoni Brichfeus, Carles Gastó et Ramon Forcada à Sant Joan Despí

1933

Innengestaltung des Gebäudes des Landwirteverbandes von Sant Joan Despí
Wohnhaus für Jaume Casas in Sant Joan Despí

Interiors for the Farmers' Union building in Sant Joan Despí
Detached house for Jaume Casas in Sant Joan Despí

Transformation de l'intérieur du bâtiment du syndicat agricole de Sant Joan Despí
Maison pour Jaume Casas à Sant Joan Despí

1934

Arbeiten an der Kirche von Roda de Barà
Wohnhaus für Miquel Vila in Sant Joan Despí

Work on Roda de Barà church
House for Miquel Vila in Sant Joan Despí

Travaux dans l'église de Roda de Barà
Maison individuelle pour Miquel Vila à Sant Joan Despí

1935

Dekorative Arbeiten für die Mas Carreras in Roda de Barà
Wohnhaus für Montserrat Batllorí Mansana in Sant Joan Despí

Decorative work for Mas Carreras in Roda de Barà
House for Montserrat Batllorí Mansana in Sant Joan Despí

Travaux décoratifs pour le Mas Carreras à Roda de Barà
Maison pour Montserrat Batllorí Mansana à Sant Joan Despí

1939

Umbau des Kollegiums des Heiligen Herzens in Tarragona (beendet 1943)
Restaurierung der Pfarrkirche von Sant Joan a Campins
Umbauentwurf für das Santa-Monica-Konvent in Barcelona

Alterations to the College of the Sacred Heart in Tarragona (completed 1943)
Restoration of the parish church of Sant Joan a Campins
Project for the redesign of the Santa Monica convent in Barcelona

Transformation du collège du Sacré-Cœur à Tarragone (terminée en 1943)
Rénovation de l'église paroissiale de Sant Joan a Campins
Projet pour la transformation de l'intérieur du couvent Santa Monica à Barcelone

1940

Chorraum der Kirche von Guimerà
Arbeiten im »Gremi de Pagesos« von Tarragona
Arbeiten an der Aula und dem Archivraum der Architekturschule in Barcelona
Umbauarbeiten in der Kirche von El Vendrell (beendet 1949)

Presbytery of the Guimerà church
Alterations to the »Gremi de Pagesos« in Tarragona
Alterations to the auditorium and archives in the College of Architecture in Barcelona
Alterations to the El Vendrell church (completed 1949)

Chœur de l'église de Guimerà
Travaux dans le »Gremi de Pagesos« de Tarragone
Transformation de la salle de lecture et des archives de l'Ecole d'architecture à Barcelone
Transformation de l'église de El Vendrell (terminée en 1949)

1941

Umbau der Kirche von Bonastre (1944 beendet)

Restoration of Bonastre church (completed 1944)

Transformation de l'église de Bonastre (terminée en 1944)

1942

Arbeiten an der Kirche Santa Maria del Pi in Barcelona
Umbauarbeiten an der Casa Solé in Els Pallaresos

Work on Santa Maria del Pi church in Barcelona
Alterations to the Casa Solé in Els Pallaresos

Travaux dans l'église Santa Maria del Pi à Barcelone
Transformation de la Casa Solé à Els Pallaresos

1943

Erweiterung des Stifts der Barmherzigen Karmeliterinnen in Tarragona
Arbeiten an der Kirche von Sant Joan Despí
Altäre der Krypta Güell (1948 fertiggestellt)
Umbauten am Torre Codina in Badalona (beendet 1947)

Extensions to the Carmelite Sisters of Mercy convent in Tarragona
Work on Sant Joan Despí church
Altars for the Güell Chapel (completed 1948)
Alterations to the Torre Codina in Badalona (completed 1947)

Agrandissement du couvent des Carmélites de la Charité de Tarragone
Travaux dans l'église de Sant Joan Despí
Autels de la crypte Güell (terminés en 1948)
Transformation de la Torre Codina à Badalona (terminée en 1947)

1944

Dekor und Umbau in der Kapelle des Mas Carreras in Roda de Barà
Dekorationen in der Kirche von Capellades

Decoration and renovation of Mas Carreras chapel in Roda de Barà
Decorations in the Capellades church

Décoration et transformation de la chapelle de Mas Carreras à Roda de Barà
Décorations de l'église de Capellades

1945

Umbauten in der Pfarrkirche von Claramunt
Altarentwürfe für die Kirche von Els Pallaresos (1947 fertiggestellt)
Arbeiten an der Sakristei und Bau der Kuppel der Kirche von Capellades (1949 beendet)

Alterations to the parish church of Claramunt
Altar design for the church of Els Pallaresos (completed 1947)
Work on the sacristy and construction of the dome for the Capellades church (completed 1949)

Transformation de l'église paroissiale de Claramunt
Projets pour l'autel de l'église de Els Pallaresos (terminés en 1947)
Travaux dans la sacristie et construction de la coupole de l'église de Capellades (terminée en 1949)

1946

Altarraum der Krankenhauskapelle von Capellades

Sanctuary of the hospital chapel in Capellades

Sanctuaire de la chapelle de l'hôpital de Capellades

1947

Glasfenster der Pfarrkirche von Vilanova i la Geltrú
Hochaltar und Chor der Kapelle im Stiftshaus von Vilanova i la Geltrú

Stained glass window for the parish church of Vilanova i la Geltrú
Main altar and choir for the Vilanova i la Geltrú convent

Vitraux de l'église paroissiale de Vilanova i la Geltrú
Maître-autel et chœur de la chapelle du couvent de Vilanova i la Geltrú

1948

Altar der Pfarrkirche von Vilanova i la Geltrú
Umbauten an der Pfarrkirche von Santa Coloma de Gramanet

Altar for the parish church of Vilanova i la Geltrú
Alterations to the parish church of Santa Coloma de Gramanet

Autel de l'église paroissiale de Vilanova i la Geltrú
Transformation de l'église paroissiale de Sante Coloma de Gramanet

1949

Jujol stirbt am 1. Mai in Barcelona
Sitz der Caixa d'Estalvis Provincial der Diputació von Barcelona in Sant Joan Despí

Jujol dies in Barcelona on 1 May
Headquarters of the Caixa d'Estalvis Provincial of the Barcelona Diputació in Sant Joan Despí

Josep Maria Jujol meurt le 1er mai à Barcelone
Siège de la Caixa d'Estalvis Provincial du conseil général de Barcelone à Sant Joan Despí

BILDNACHWEIS / CREDITS / CREDITS PHOTOGRAPHIQUES

Die Fotografien von Jordi Sarrà wurden ergänzt durch Aufnahmen von Ferran Freixa, Barcelona (S. 13, 133, 137), Lluís Casals, Barcelona (S. 68/69), Peter Gössel, Nürnberg (S. 98), sowie Zeichnungen und historische Aufnahmen aus dem Arxiu Jujol, Barcelona, dem Arxiu del Collegi d'Arquitectes de Catalunya, Barcelona, dem Arxiu Municipal de Sant Joan Despí und dem Cátedra Gaudí Archiv, Barcelona; die Reproduktionen stammen von cb foto, Barcelona, Lluís Casals, Barcelona, und Foto Krauss, Nürnberg.

The photographs by Jordi Sarrà were supplemented with pictures taken by Ferran Freixa, Barcelona (p. 13, 133, 137), Lluís Casals, Barcelona (p. 68/69), Peter Gössel, Nuremberg (p. 98), as well as drawings and historical photos from the Arxiu Jujol, Barcelona, the Arxiu del Collegi d'Arquitectes de Catalunya, Barcelona, the Arxiu Municipal de Sant Joan Despí and the Cátedra Gaudí Archive, Barcelona; the reproductions were provided by cb foto, Barcelona, Lluís Casals , Barcelona, and Foto Krauss, Nuremberg.

Outre les photographies de Jordi Sarrà, mentionnons celles réalisées par Ferran Freixa, Barcelone (p. 13, 133, 137), Lluís Casals, Barcelone (p. 68/69), Peter Gössel, Nuremberg (p. 98), ainsi que les dessins et les photographies historiques du Arxiu Jujol, Barcelone, du Arxiu del Collegi d'Arquitectes de Catalunya, Barcelone, du Arxiu Municipal de Sant Joan Despí et des Archives Cátedra Gaudí, Barcelone; les reproductions proviennent de cb foto, Barcelone, Lluís Casals, Barcelone, et de Foto Krauss, Nuremberg.